The Downsizing of America

THE DOWNSIZING OF AMERICA

RONALD AYLING

NOVA SCIENCE PUBLISHERS, INC.
COMMACK, NY

Creative Design: Gavin Aghamore
Editorial Production: Susan Boriotti
Art Director: Maria Ester Hawrys
Assistant Director: Elenor Kallberg
Graphics: Frank Grucci
Manuscript Coordinator: Phyllis Gaynor
Book Production: Joanne Bennette, Michelle Keller
                     Christine Mathosian and Tammy Sauter
Circulation: Iyatunde Abdullah, Cathy DeGregory and Annette Hellinger

Library of Congress Cataloging-in-Publication Data
available upon request

ISBN 1-50672-431-5

Copyright © 1997 by Nova Science Publishers, Inc.
               6080 Jericho Turnpike, Suite 207
               Commack, New York 11725
               Tele. 516-499-3103   Fax 516-499-3146
               E-mail: Novascience@earthlink.net

All rights reserved. No part of this book may be reproduced, stored in a retrieval system or transmitted in any form or by any means: electronic, electrostatic, magnetic, tape, mechanical photocopying, recording or otherwise without permission from the publishers.

The authors and publisher haven taken care in preparation of this book, but make no expressed or implied warranty of any kind and assume no responsibility for any errors or omissions. No liability is assumed for incidental or consequential damages in connection with or arising out of information contained in this book.

This publication is designed to provide accurate and authoritative information with regard to the subject matter covered herein. It is sold with the clear understanding that the publisher is not engaged in rendering legal or any other professional services. If legal or any other expert assistance is required, the services of a competent person should be sought. FROM A DECLARATION OF PARTICIPANTS JOINTLY ADOPTED BY A COMMITTEE OF THE AMERICAN BAR ASSOCIATION AND A COMMITTEE OF PUBLISHERS.

Printed in the United States of America

CONTENTS

Part 1 Downsizing - What it is and What Steps can be Taken Instead of Downsizing..................1

1.	Introduction	3
2.	Downsizing	11
3.	Steps to Improve Cash Flow	15
4.	Management	21
5.	Communications	27
6.	Technology	37
7.	Re-structuring	43
8.	Fragmentation	47
9.	Mistakes	53
10.	Labor Changes	61
11.	Re-engineering	67
12.	Looking after the Customer	73
13.	Conclusion	79

Part 2 How to use the "Human" Resource as the Valuable Asset that it is! 81

14.	Introduction 83
15.	Use the "Human" Resource 85
16.	Set the Employees Free 95
17.	Leadership 103
18.	Regain Employee Confidence 107
19.	Staff at the Correct Level 111
20.	Develop a Strong Sense of Direction 117
21.	Develop and Use Internal Talents 123
22.	Use Talent Innovatively 129
23.	Grow Employees in Place 135
24.	Eliminate Excessive Administrative Work 141
25.	Add Employees to your Management Team 147
26.	Make Ethics a Cornerstone of your Business 151
27.	Summation - Why Corporations will Stop Downsizing 155
28.	Conclusion 165

Addendum 169

Bibliography 171

Glossary 173

Index 175

PART 1

DOWNSIZING - WHAT IT IS AND WHAT STEPS CAN BE TAKEN INSTEAD OF DOWNSIZING

1. Introduction

Corporations are the modern business armies that carry their products and services to international economic battlefields, where these products or services compete against other nations' corporate products. Companies and corporations that strive to sell their products and services, do so for one purpose: To make a profit! Without that profit, they would wither and eventually cease to exist, at least in their present form.

So profit-making companies and corporations are *social* organizations whose only reason for existence is to make a profit. Profit, or the lack of it, is the harsh and final judgment of all the collective dreams, aspirations, and efforts of all of the company's employees.

The management of any company can have the best laid plans and ideas but without the effort and assistance of its employees, it will fail. Conversely, the most motivated and energetic corporate employees with poor management and weak direction are also doomed to failure.

Is it surprising when companies with superb products and unsurpassed customer services falter? Probably not any more than a company with a mediocre product or service that succeeds wildly!

By examining the above, you may conclude that it is not a product or products, nor is it a service or services which is vital to a company's success. Of course, it must have a combination of good products and service and the active support of skilled and motivated employees to have continuing success.

This may seem, and is, elementary! However, many corporations in existence today seem to have forgotten that the company is more than a sum of its newest products or its latest service. Those alone will not make them successful: **It is also and especially, its people.**

HISTORY

All corporations and companies in existence today had their beginnings in the minds and skills of a small group of people. As the idea that the company was founded to develop grew into a product or products, the company grew in size as it was nurtured by the skills and efforts of the few pioneers that started it. Each employee was a vital part of the new company, fitting into place like a missing puzzle piece. To make the company successful, employees worked together, solving the problems of the growing organization. Problem solving was accomplished quickly by the person that recognized the problem going directly to the person that designed or developed the product or service. The direct feedback of any problems (and possible solutions), led to quick problem resolution.

Employees were driven by the ideas that formed the new company. Like a dream, these concepts led them on. The pay that they received was a mere facet of their reward; they were part of a dream! All but the most callous caught a bit of the dream - it guided them onward like a beckoning light. The first months of the new company turned into years; the challenges grew and were overcome. Then, some years later, they all realized that the dream that they had worked for had become reality. Along with that reality came growth, success, and more growth, until the few visionaries were supplemented by new employees with less of the original dream.

Eventually, when the company grew to a larger size, some of the original founders retired or were replaced by less inspired employees, until the original company became unrecognizable. Many people now just worked for a salary. They had little idea of how they fitted into the plans and goals of the organization. They just did their job to the extent of their supervisor's wishes and their own personal levels of motivation. Some did well to grow, develop and progress within the organization. Others did well to satisfy their own sense of job satisfaction. Still others just went along for the ride, (and the pay).

For many years, corporations were the paths to success and prosperity for many workers at all levels. They were also, collectively, the strength that provided national pride and power in world markets and also equipment and supplies in wars and conflicts. Companies have never been perfect, being the social organizations that they are, they suffer from the imperfect directions of ego-driven humans. But, for the most part, many peoples' dreams were realized through their work for these corporations.

THE PRESENT

From the seventies onward, and particularly during the 1990's, an alarming trend in corporate culture has taken place. To improve their profit margins, many companies began restructuring and reducing the number of their employees. This was necessary and imperative in a few cases as some companies had become top-heavy with too many employees in certain areas to be economically efficient. In times of strong economic growth, some companies loosen financial controls and employee hiring practices so that when the inevitable economic downturns occur, they are left overstaffed and over-budgeted. The most common reaction to poor economic performance and stock market pressure caused by this overstaffing is, of course, elimination of staff.

The reality is that many of these downsizings often ignore the basic premise of preserving those employees that directly impact revenue and are economically justified. Many unfortunate cases have occurred when employees vital to a company's success have been put out of work while other employees in overstaffed or unnecessary administrative functions have been retained.

Companies often create unnecessary administrative tasks and requirements, with associated administrators to file and study mountains of data that are only of limited benefit to the company's ultimate success. Yet, these departments are often spared when reductions take place, while employees more central to cash generation are removed. Rather than precisely trimming the overstaffing that exists, often a haphazard reduction of employees takes place that impacts the effectiveness of the organization to conduct business at the current level and certainly deters any efforts to grow and develop new business.

Also, some organizations suffer from duplication of effort, unresponsive administrative functions, and less than effective communications systems. These all cause inefficiencies that slow down the flow of business. These may appear as small items but collectively they can have major impact on day-to-day business efforts.

Many corporations go from one restructuring plan to another, laying off employees and reorganizing departments. When this reduction does not provide the results desired, yet another round of restructuring / downsizing is begun. This, of course leads to further inefficiencies and poorer economic performance. Along with the poorer economic performance goes worsening worker morale, fear, and insecurity.

Like many trends that start and take place for necessary reasons, this trend has gained a life of its own as corporations strive to gain stock market approval by their re-structuring / reorganization plans. Read any paper or listen to any news broadcast and you will see company after company shedding employees like a dieter sheds excess pounds.

In many cases, even companies with good cash-flows resort to downsizing to try to drive their apparent value, (and consequently, stock values), higher. Often, any stock market gains that result are short-lived because when the effect of the latest reduction in force begins permeating the organization, long term company success suffers.

In virtually every case, the employees that remain must do more just to cover the workload of the workers that have left. Overtime is up, employee morale is down, and customer satisfaction will begin to suffer. This should be obvious!

What is less obvious is the stifling of employee growth in a downsized company. A company that is smaller in size needs fewer managers and other upper level employees and thus provides less opportunities for growth for lower level workers. Also, as middle management is always a prime target for any restructuring, many lower level employees are deterred from striving for advancement out of fear of future downsizing.

Couple this with the very real fear for one's job, the frustration and anger of seeing valued coworkers leave, and a deep distrust for anything the corporation says or does, and you begin to see the dissatisfaction that is almost epidemic in corporations today.

As indicated above, downsizing companies are freezing growth paths and eliminating the growth and development of promising employees. This also prevents the flow of new ideas and the influx of new upper level managers with recent low level experience. This leads to calcified upper management whose ideas may not reflect current reality at lower levels of the corporation and to poor decisions based on out of date assumptions of reality.

Another trend that is becoming common in many corporations currently is the practice of outsourcing or contracting out many of the functions that were formerly part of the corporation. Of course, there are some functions that should be outsourced. A prime example of one function that could be is the computer department, or management information system, (M.I.S.)

In some companies, the data processing function has become so specialized and multi-faceted that those companies do not have the talents or the overall knowledge to provide cost-effective data processing services to the organization. Look at the M.I.S. department of many companies and you see a department that is out of control. Network development, rapid growth of PC use, and ever increasing demand for storage capacity has stretched the ability of management to control equipment and software costs within the organization and the resources to support them almost beyond reason. Largely uncontrolled equipment and software growth has caused a financial drain that could bring all but the largest company to economic ruin.

Outsourcing the entire data processing function to a company that specializes in data processing is a way to control rampant equipment and software growth. This way the company could control the cash flow and also the direction that its data processing effort is heading. But unlike the example just mentioned, most of the departments in a typical corporation work better and are more responsive if they are part of the corporation and are not contracted out.

The current corporate "buzz-word" is "core business." Core business is the primary revenue generating function of a particular business. Many other corporate functions are being off-loaded to contractors as though that panacea will solve all the company's problems. It is very important to evaluate each function and its worth to the corporation before contracting that service out as some loss of control goes with each department that is sub-contracted. Sub-contracting creates many problems of control and also of hidden costs that only become apparent when the outsourcing has taken place. It also creates considerable morale problems for the remaining employees when working with less responsive and less concerned contract workers.

THE FUTURE

What does the future hold for companies and corporations and their employees? Will the corporations become mere cores served by contractors and sub-contractors? Will employees shed by the companies have to work for sub-contractors with a decreased level of pay and little or no health or other benefits? Is this where the Great American Dream is leading? Will continued employee displacement and decreased pay eventually lead to lower consumer demand and even more stringent corporate belt-tightening and employee displacement until a severe economic recession or depression takes place.

WHY WORRY ABOUT CORPORATIONS

There are those that might ask, "why worry about companies and corporations?" "What does it matter if they fall into decline as the best and brightest employees tire of making sense of corporate cultures and spin off into their own businesses?"

We all should care and be concerned! Large healthy corporations are very important to our national economic health. Small businesses, regardless of how successful they are, cannot compete against huge foreign corporations. These large foreign corporations which are often government subsidized, have already given corporate America a wake-up call with their floods of high quality and low priced goods.

Like them or not, large corporations are necessary to our continued success as a powerful nation of independent people. If foreign corporations gain ascendancy, the power that follows that success will flow elsewhere, much to our detriment.

The question is not, should we try to make corporations work, but how can we?

2. Downsizing

As previously discussed, the reasons that are given by companies for downsizing could be: To reduce excess overhead, to improve economic performance, and to positively affect stock market value.

It can take place as plant closures, as reductions in the number of staff, consolidation of departments, or as widespread individual layoffs. Some more benign aspects of downsizing are early retirements or employee buy-outs with some economic package to encourage participation. More often, it is the unexpected and sudden announcement of terminations.

Sometimes, like a silent thief, it steals through the company and removes friends, acquaintances, and work-mates. It is only by rumors and half-twisted truths that one finds out when a trusted fellow worker is gone. This type of reduction is the most deadly and the most worrisome. It is so because the deadly tentacles of downsizing mandates reach quietly out to remove one after another business friend. This form of downsizing is like a hidden Gestapo, just waiting to strike. Only the privileged few know where and when this scourge will strike again or how long it will go on for. The remainder of the work force have the threat of this dangling "Sword of Damocles" overhead, constantly threatening, always promising to fall.

Whatever face downsizing takes, it has the destructive effect of a severe blow to the confidence of dismissed employees and widespread lack of trust in remaining employees. No person can take a personal major blow such as caused by a sudden, unexpected lay-off, without having massive self-doubts and rapid destruction of one's self-esteem. Whatever pretty face that the human resource department tries to put on downsizing, it is a very negative and destructive action that impacts not only the removed employees and their families but the ones that remain. It spreads the poison of doubt and fear throughout the company, creating distrust and suspicion in its wake.

With the larger size of companies and the reduction of personal contact between management and employees that implies; downsizing becomes a highly impersonal action, with little care for the well-being of the many trusting and dedicated employees. Employees might as well be part of a job loss lottery as management sits around the polished tables, making plans that cause anguish and despair to the unfortunate workers selected for dismissal.

How can the persons that are responsible for making such decisions calmly continue on as though downsizing is just another management action, like changing the color of the paint on cafeteria walls? Many people have to go through an unwarranted and undeserved hell to struggle to try to put their lives back together after they have been blown asunder by these callous actions. It is obvious that the consciences of these "captains of industry" that lay the scourge of unwarranted downsizings on their companies are woefully deficient.

Rather than just an impersonal dismissal of a number of employees to meet a goal, downsizing is an action that causes employees major personal problems. Aside from the obvious blow to self-esteem are added the hidden effects of family upheaval, monetary problems, relocation, depression, family break-ups, and worse.

For this reason downsizing is not a step that should be taken lightly. All other steps that can be taken to improve efficiency and economic performance should be exhausted before resorting to reductions of staff levels. As stated in other chapters, downsizing should be utilized as a last ditch act of desperation to save a bankrupt company. It should not be used as an economic tool to try to fix economic shortcomings. These shortcomings will still exist after downsizing, so that the long term success of companies will become even more elusive.

It is time that management of companies stopped thinking about the next quarter and started thinking about making their companies successful for the long term. If they did, they would see that, with few exceptions, downsizing does not have a place in those long term plans.

Other steps to optimize performance are listed in the following chapters. These chapters examine some of the inefficiencies that are common in most organizations. These inefficiencies often develop because of poor direction, company growth, increase of technology etc. Individually, they may seem minor in nature but the overall impact may be the difference between failure, just breaking even, or making a profit.

3. Steps to Improve Cash Flow

Since a for-profit corporation is by definition a social organization whose aim is to make a profit, let's begin at the heart of the matter .... profit!

Over-head

If profit is the aim of an organization, that organization should constantly strive to keep costs and overhead low. You might think that the average corporation with its brigades of accountants would do well here! Not necessarily so! But many of the failures that are blamed on the accountants are unfair. Of course, the accountants are merely tools that are used by corporate management, so they are in most cases only doing what they are told. They are not responsible for the direction or style of the corporation. These things are dictated by corporate officers.

For example, many companies exist in a feast or famine environment. When cash flow into a company is high, often financial management is loosened, excess employees are hired and new functions are put into place, often without sound financial reasoning. Later, when economic downturns take place, this results in a scramble to the side of financial austerity. During this latter time, employee reductions also occur, often in areas that should be staffed at present sizes or even increased in size.

Any company should be as stringent during strong positive cash flow situations as it is in negative cash flow periods. It is always easy to hire new employees; it is always very difficult to ask them to leave if they have been doing their job well.

Most sales and service functions have some form of revenue per employee basis that is or should be, adhered to. Administrative overhead is an area that has less direct economic control and is commonly the area that grows for other than sound economic reasons. These reasons may be power struggles, new directions, empire building or just vague overhead drift. Whatever the reasoning, employee growth should be scrutinised very carefully to make sure that it makes economic sense.

Duplication of effort is another area that can be addressed to eliminate unnecessary overhead. Often, direct duplication of effort is not a problem because it is so obvious. More often problems occur when two functions overlap and create duplication of effort. Aside from the obvious redundancy of effort caused by these overlaps, they also create added confusion and slow down administrative efficiency.

Another area of unneeded overhead is decentralization of functions. Some functions, of course, need to be decentralized to be effective. Others, such as those that deal with cash flow and financial decisions are often more efficient if centralized. A good rule of thumb is determining whether to centralize functions or not is the decision level of the function. If the department or function can make all relevant decisions at that level and it makes sense to have it at a lower level, it should be. If, however, many of the decisions must be made at a higher level, the department should be centralized. This should improve standardization and service and cut down duplication of effort.

Sound business practice should also prevent costly cross-functional operations. Out-of-area operations that entail high transportation costs should be eliminated. An example of this would be a sales manager selling equipment in another area but providing continuing support from a local area. If the business is sound, the sale should be made but support should come from the other area.

ACCOUNTS RECEIVABLE

This is an area that most companies could improve upon! Often, too little attention is given to the monthly revenues flowing in from customers. This is money that the company is owed! The highest priority should be given to reduce outstanding accounts receivable to the minimum amount possible.

Companies should strongly reaffirm guide-lines for customer billing for services and provide first level managers with tools to monitor revenue. Also financial departments should be provided with directions to monitor and control accounts receivable quickly. Often one must overcome financial department inertia to correct incorrect or faulty billing situations. This should not happen!

Financial lines of communication are, and should be treated as, the most important communication that takes place within a company. These lines are so vital because they supply the cash flow that is the very life blood of the organization. Any company that allows these lines to become inefficient will become less successful because cash flow will be slowed.

REVENUE CONTROL

One mistake that many growing companies make is to place less importance on low level revenue control. The tool that is very effective in monitoring revenue and expenses is the quarterly presentation.

The quarterly presentation is, of course, a regular "state of economic health" for each department, large or small. If used correctly with data gathered from corporate databases, it can give a snapshot of current economic health of a department and any financial variances or anomalies.. If the same format is used regularly, a historical pattern can be displayed to analyse growth areas and areas of higher expenses. Using the trends provided by this historical prospective, departments can analyse revenue growth and expenses. The trends also provide a very sound basis for preparing a realistic budget for following periods.

A corporate officer should be able to sit in on any level of quarterly presentation and understand and evaluate the performance of that presentation. This can only be done if a company-wide standard for quarterly presentations is adhered to and is based on corporate revenue and expenditures for each department.

The quarterly presentation highlights areas of weaknesses and can be used to improve control in most cases. Some departments will, of course have some economic shortfalls that are caused by corporate decisions. For example, a service organization might be required to take on uneconomic situations because of a nation-wide agreement with a large customer.

Since a company is no more than a large number of small departments, it is vital that the economic performance of the lowest levels be optimised by realistic evaluations. Too often dictates from above direct lower level functions with little or no feedback from those levels, often with poor results.

It is important to get the lowest department levels running correctly before going upward and evaluating other levels. Too often as companies grow, attention to lower level department performance diminishes, with lost revenue resulting.

For example, a computer manufacturing and service company should conduct a yearly audit to verify installed machines and all installed features. After completing this, an accountant or other financial assistant should work with each manager to verify that service charges are correct for each customer.

This information should be entered into a database that provides each manager with an exact account of service revenue that is generated from those accounts, be it service contract revenue, relocations, etc. The database should also key on contract expirations or warranty expirations so that renewal efforts can be made before any expirations occur.

This income is the easiest for the company to retain as the customer already has purchased the product or service but in some companies, is taken for granted. This must not be allowed! Protection of existing revenue protects the company's long term success!

Uneconomic Situations

Sometimes companies have to do things to get a sale in a particular area that are not economically sound. This could be to open a new service area with insufficient revenue to justify it. If this is done, all effort must be made to grow the area until it becomes financially viable.

Often, a company may choose to take a loss or break even in a particular market segment if it will provide increased customer sales potential. This is good business practice if a firm plan exists that ensures that full advantage is gained from these "loss leaders." Strong sales management can ensure that the proper emphasis is placed on these situations to take advantage of the position gained by placing low income items in a particular market place.

Too often, situations are allowed to continue that create a cash drain on company resources. They should either be rectified by sales efforts or eliminated! Each situation should be evaluated if it falls outside normal company guidelines to measure the total impact to company revenue. Then if the situation makes sound business sense for the company, the decision should be made to go ahead with the business.

False Economies

Sometimes area managers will make decisions that will look good for short term financial considerations but are poor long term business practices.

An example of this could be an area manager demanding that his employees drive to far flung parts of his area, rather than flying. This saves the cost of an airline ticket but increases costs for travel and hotel as well as increases time that the employee is unavailable for his normal work.

Another example could be that a service manager could choose not to send his technicians to training courses. Of course, he will save the cost of training but the company will incur increased overtime and customer down-times because of poor training. It also implies higher customer dissatisfaction.

Too often decisions are made to impact the immediate (quarterly), bottom line of the particular area, to make an individual or small group *look* better. Decisions should be made that are in the company's best long term interest or rather than to allow decisions that provide short lived advantages to individuals or small groups but that are detrimental to overall company profit or loss.

The title of this segment could be titled "Accountants Rule," because many blame accountants or the financial department for a company's poor performance. Accountants are merely tools of management! **It is the management's responsibility to use the financial department to focus on areas to improve the profit Vs loss performance.**

4. MANAGEMENT

Much can be done to improve the effectiveness of management. In many companies, many levels of management are not as efficient as they could be for many reasons.

For many companies, lower level management has become a position that has a great deal of responsibility but little or no authority. First level management has responsibility because the management often deals directly with customers. Consequently, these managers are directly accountable for customer satisfaction, even though many of the factors that impact this may be outside their control.

Managers, at any level, must have some authority over, or at least some input on, the factors that affect the success of their department. If they cannot affect decisions that are made that cause impact on the revenues and expenses governing their department, they become mere rubber stamp managers with little control over their success or failure. These unfortunate managers will, of course, be held to task for any failures or short-comings but can have little real impact on the outcome other than managing the resources at their disposal.

An example of this would be the service manager of a company that sells large home appliances. A problem would occur if that company allowed its sales representatives to sell machines far outside the normal service area. This would require the service manager's technicians to spend more time traveling and less working, which would drive up travel expenses, repair costs, and probably overtime.

Another example would be if the same company allowed the sales representatives to sell extended maintenance coverage for the same price as a normal service contract. Of course, this would cut directly into the service manager's profits by increasing costs without increasing revenue.

Of course, these are decisions that could be made to increase competitiveness, increase sales, etc. Most companies would not allow sales representatives to make sales outside of normal guidelines without considering the overall cost to the company and without increasing the service manager's revenue to reflect the increased workload, so that he / she could hire extra people. This would allow the same level of service to existing customers, as well as the ability to cope with new service contracts.

Short Term Management

Some companies have become so enamoured with stock performance that many management decisions are short term, in other words, designed to make company quarterly performance look good. While no company with publicly traded stock can ignore stock prices, these short term decisions are often detrimental to long term company success.

An example using the above company that sells home appliances could be the decision of the service manager not to train his / her technicians on new equipment. Of course, he / she would save the cost of travel, hotel bills, meals, and the cost of the training.

Long term, of course, this would not make sense as the technicians would take much longer to repair the new equipment, which would drive up maintenance costs and lead to dissatisfied customers.

Economic Performance Monitoring

Of course upper management, if astute to the state of their business, would monitor quarterly presentations and notice anomalies such as stated above.

A constant evaluation of each department's performance is no less important in a large corporation than in a small company. Of course, poor economic performance may take longer to affect the company's economic health but widespread poor performance will have the same end result.

MICROMANAGEMENT

Another area that constrains management is micromanagement. This occurs when an upper level manager either distrusts his subordinates or thinks that he can manager better than they can.

The lower level manager will be bombarded by requests and demands, leaving little time to do the job that the company pays him / her to do; manage. If the reason for micromanagement is a sub-standard manager, he / she should be assisted until he / she improves, or is removed if he / she doesn't improve.

A manager that micromanages wastes a great deal of time and often confuses and frustrates lower level managers that report to him / her. These micromanagers are often "managers on the make." In other words, they are striving to impress more senior management with their activity levels. Unfortunately, these micromanagers by their intrusion into decisions that should be delegated to a lower level, slow the decision making process and create confusion.

CONFUSED OR CONVOLUTED REPORTING STRUCTURES

More often than companies would like to admit, restructuring causes confused reporting structures with uncertain authority and decision levels. This leads to a lot of buck passing as no one is really sure what decisions he / she can make.

Any structural changes should be accompanied by firm guidelines to guide the level of decision making at each level and who should make those decisions. Otherwise what happens is that one must talk to many different persons before the correct person is reached that can and will, make the appropriate decision.

LACK OF LOWER LEVEL INVOLVEMENT

Many companies suffer because they have too little involvement of lower levels of the company in decision making or planning for the future. As companies are changing more rapidly to remain competitive, it is more important today to have shop floor involvement in company decisions.

For reasons given in previous chapters, the flow of new managers up through the company has slowed or stopped. This has led to top managers that are progressively further out of touch with day-to-day operations. It is vital to have direct input from shop floor and other low levels to provide a desperately needed touch of reality to the decision making process.

There are employees out there in each company with ideas for new business and solutions to old problems; they just must be given a chance to voice their ideas.

I know the comment will be raised "my company already has a suggestion program." Unfortunately, most suggestion programs are weak reflections of what they should be. Employees have learned in the past that innovative or incisive ideas are largely met by indifference. Consequently good ideas are lost because they are not paid the proper attention by upper management.

An example is a suggestion in the shipping department that could have saved one company one million dollars per year. The suggester was given his recognition and the corporate officer was effusive with his praise. After the fanfare died down and the suggester had spent his reward, the shipping department gradually digressed back to the old, more expensive way of doing business and gradually ignored the suggested improvement.

If you examine the human reactions involved, you begin to realize why the idea failed. Of course, the suggester was pleased with the attention. His coworkers were doubtless jealous or envious. The suggester's manager was quietly angry and also fearful that someone would realize he, as manager, should have figured out the less expensive solution. As a result, more people in the shipping department wanted the idea to fail and besides, it was more work.

Another way that the reward could have been handled, rather than just rewarding one person, is that the reward could have been given to the entire department: For example, if 1% of the actual amount saved was given to the suggester, 1/2% was given to the manager and 3 1/2% shared across the rest of the department. These amounts could be paid when actual savings were realized. That way, everyone in the department would have a reason to support the idea. Now the company would be saving *one million dollars every year*, (or 950,000 dollars after the rewards were made), rather than zero!

As stated previously, in the average company there are people that have ideas that can save or make money for that company. It is up to management to recognize and create an environment that such people could be comfortable and develop their ideas into real savings. For those doubting persons that still feel that their suggestion or quality programs address the above, anonymously submit an idea to your suggestion program and see how far it gets!

GREAT LEAP FORWARD

Many companies of necessity must plan into the future to develop new products and strategies so they are not left standing by more astute competition. This is as it should be. What often happens is that these plans that focus a company's direction in a certain way that may be proven to be unrealistic as time progresses.

Unfortunately, some companies treat these long term plans as "Holy Grails" and cling to plans that diverge from reality. Plans are and should be flexible! Change is the every day currency of any corporation. Any plan or idea that is shown to fail the test of reality as time passes should be altered or discarded as the situation demands. Any company that bases their decisions on a skewed picture of reality must suffer the economic consequences.

DIVERGENT DIRECTIONS

Companies come into being with a strong direction of what they are and what they do and where they want to go.

As companies grow, they often diverge from their "core" success area because of takeovers, mergers or just taking new directions for the future.

Unfortunately many takeovers or mergers take a company in new directions that their base expertise and skills has not prepared them for. A totally different mindset may be necessary to be successful in the new area but unfortunately, many companies try to bend the new acquisition to their own mindset and values.

The result is a less successful operation at best or a sickly cash drain that weakens the original financially sound company. It is presumptuous to assume that tactics and procedures that were successful in the original company will also lead to success in new areas.

There are successful companies in each area of the market. It would be good to examine their strategies and tactics to see how they are successful in that area before plunging unawares into a new endeavour in a new area.

In the competitive environment that exists in business today, managers need all the assistance that they can get in managing day-to-day and long term operations. Often, the assistance is there in the abilities and talents of their employees. The astute companies have, and will continue to utilize this largely untapped resource.

5. Communications

At the heart of every company is some form of communications system. It could be telephone, meetings, word-of-mouth, or one of the many more modern communications systems. Whatever system is used, most companies could improve their efficiency by improving their communications.

To put this in prospective, you may remember the old parlour game that starts a phrase at one side of the room. By the time that the phrase is passed to the other side of the room, the phrase has completely changed. We each put our own interpretation or slant on ideas that we receive and pass that on. Add into this mix; ego, concern, power struggles, etc., and it is a wonder that we are able to communicate at all. Throw in modern technology and new communications systems and we shouldn't be surprised that poor communications exists in most companies in spite of the latest communications technology.

Telephone answering systems, voice mail, paging systems, telephone conferencing, video conferencing, fax, and e-mail systems are some of the newer communications systems that are available to speed up and improve communications. However, it is possible to abuse each system and to make them less effective.

For example: Many companies have installed phone direction systems that utilise some form of answering system / voice mail that is intended to respond more effectively to phone calls if the person called is away from his / her desk or is unavailable. Unfortunately, these systems are often used by employees to filter phone calls or to bypass answering calls.

For example, every time that one attempts to contact a person, all that one gets is a recording with the message that they are not at their desk. While these voice mail / answering machines are good if a person is truly unavailable or busy, some people are notorious for not answering their phones or returning calls, even when they are available. Persons not responding to calls or not returning them causes repetitive wasted calls. No person in a position to conduct telephone business, either with internal employees or with customers, should be allowed to defer telephone calls in this manner.

Another problem that can occur because of these voice mail / answering systems is "phone tag." Of course, this takes place if the telephone call that you made earlier is returned when you are out of the office or unable to return the call. This leads to several calls from both parties until you are able to get through and discuss what may have been a simple request or question.

One reason that this happens is if the original caller leaves his or her work area just after leaving a phone message, so that when their call is returned within a reasonable time, they are not around to receive the call. It is important to remain near your telephone for a half hour, if possible, when you have left a message and expect a return call. Conversely, the person called should make all efforts to return the call within the half hour, otherwise the original caller may have left his or her work area.

An even worse problem than "phone tag" is "dead silence." After a message is left when the called party is not available, nothing is heard from them. When you finally get them several days later, they say that they weren't sure what you wanted. (Of course, they could have called you as you requested and they would have found out!) Misuse of telephone answering systems circumvents the added productivity that these systems could provide. It would seem reasonable that any person whose primary function is to conduct business over the telephone, should respond immediately to at least fifty per cent of the incoming calls. The remainder of the calls should be returned within thirty minutes. For important functions, assistants should be trained to cover the primary person's calls if he or she in unavailable. Important business functions should not slow down or stop because of poor telephone answering habits, policies, or the unavailability of individuals.

Another example of communications system abuse is incorrect e-mail use. Some people, when given access to e-mail, think that it is a forum for their problems and they blanket the e-mail system with memos or questionnaires. Most people that receive these "blanket" meaningless memos delete them immediately. Of course, one must first read the memo to make sure that it is in fact, "meaningless" before deleting it. If these memos are sent to large numbers of people, it wastes an inordinate amount of time for each person to read and then delete the said memos.

Another problem that occurs with e-mail systems is the redundant forwarder. This person, usually a manager, receives an e-mail and without looking at who it is copied to, immediately forwards it to his or her subordinates. If the subordinate had already received a copy from the original sender, they now have a duplicate copy that must be read to verify that it is not a change from the original.

Of course, any system of communication can be abused but the simplicity of sending multiple people memos by addressing groups of people that is one of the benefits of e-mail, also creates the strong probability that it will be misused.

E-mail now places most employees in a common communications medium. This does not in itself improve communications at all levels because communications normally takes place within a level and only small amounts of communication takes place above and below that level. Of course, top management of a company cannot correspond with even a fraction of the employees of that company and still hope to do any other meaningful work. What would be helpful would be to develop "focal points" at each level that could supplement the normal employee to manager communication. The reason for this is that too often, layers of management "filter" points of discussion by putting their own importance and interpretation of problems and solutions. Hence, many problems that could be solved earlier are not because of this "translation." What may be a serious problem may have little of the original verbiage or reasoning attached to it when it reaches the top, (if it does!) Consequently, companies must do better at building multiple lines of communications so that if one line fails to pass on problems and solutions, another line is available that may do so. These lines should be from knowledgeable persons directly to persons in a position to view the seriousness of a problem and to take steps to rectify it.

To take advantage of the new systems of communications that are now available, companies must re-evaluate their communications systems so that full advantage can be gained from the new systems. This implies changing drastically the way that companies communicate today. The companies that develop innovative means of communicating will improve their competitive edge, while other companies that resist change will founder.

Many of the problems discussed above result from giving employees new communications systems without any discussion of the proper, (and improper) uses of those systems. It would be beneficial for companies to train employees on new communications systems and to have standards of expectations for users of these systems. Along those lines, it would be beneficial to have managers discuss these standards with their subordinates so that employees were not just handed the new systems and expected to use them correctly. The example of the answering system is just one instance. What may be acceptable for home use of an answering system may be totally unacceptable in a business environment.

In addition to the modern communications systems discussed above are the more familiar modes of communication: Memos, status presentations, telephone verbal communications, meetings, and questionnaires.

Memos

Memos are the most common form of day-to-day communications and the most abused. Like any form of communication, to be effective, a memo should be concise, accurate, and understandable. In addition, memos should be to highlight a problem or define a procedure. Some managers generate memos until their subordinates are drowning in paper. For a memo to be effective, it should be important. If the item being discussed is less important, it should be handled with a more informal means of communication, such as the telephone call or normal conversation.

STATUS PRESENTATION

This is a snapshot of the current performance of a department or organisational function. They should be precise, consistent and factual. A company should have a standard presentation that provides who, what, where, how, why, and how much. For example, a quarterly presentation for a department should include employees in the department, customers, revenue produced / spent, expenses, problems, anomalies, etc. The reason these should be standardised is so that company officers can visit any department presentation and see the same type of presentation using similar facts and figures. Also, since most of the figures are provided by the company data bases, a standard presentation gives a constant that others can evaluate.

Too often managers like to embellish their presentations to show this or present that and add to basic presentations. Sometimes the result is confusion, particularly if the contents of the quarterly presentation is changed from quarter to quarter. To have value, a quarterly presentation should be constant so that it can be compared to past performance to note anomalies and indicate growth and financial performance.

A quarterly presentation that is without a constant historical context is meaningless! It is like a single picture of a person labeled "Dieter's progress." Just like the picture has no meaning without other pictures to show the person's weight loss, so must a quarterly presentation be compared to previous quarters and previous years. Any good quarterly presentation should have an absolute profit and loss comparison if the organisation is a revenue producing centre or a budget and loss, if not. Only then can a real idea of the financial soundness of the department or organisation be gained.

Telephone Conversations

Phone conversations are to pass or gather information. Some people can transact telephone business quickly and effectively, others spend much longer in phone conversations and achieve less. Of course, in addition to transacting business, one must include some brief comments of politeness and friendliness. The point is, get the business done, be polite and then get off the phone. An effective way to guide a telephone conversation is to jot down key points of the call before it is made. That way, one can refer to the notes to make sure that all points are covered and that the call is not a meandering discussion that misses one or more vital points.

Phone bills are good indicators of telephone habits. If some individuals always take much longer on each conversation on average than their peers, they may be spending too much time on phone calls and perhaps would benefit from a course on effective phone use. If managers themselves realise that they should be more effective in phone use, they should utilise tactful techniques to get off the phone more quickly and use notes to cover important points.

Verbal Communication

We all talk more than we listen. In addition to being fairly poor listeners, we filter or deflect conversations as other pressing problems tug at our consciousness. Consequently, we often miss the intent or the subtle nuance of a conversation.

If we are listening intently, we hear and should repeat to ensure that we understand what was said. We will also catch what isn't said or what may be implied by the way something is said, the tone of voice, the look on the speaker's face, etc. Voice communications is a combination of many signals that we must listen and observe to understand. We all become too busy or too self-involved to catch the meanings of conversations. How many times have we ignored a conversation, only to remember later that "he / she told me that." Too often, I would guess! By not listening better, we are less effective as communicators than we could be.

MEETINGS

Most people in companies large and small, hate meetings. They dislike them because they are very often wasteful and counter-productive. To be effective, a meeting should have an agenda or points to be discussed that should be adhered to. Meeting attendees should all have copies of the meeting so that they can be prepared to participate meaningfully.

Also, the meeting should have a goal or purpose. If the meeting does not have a goal or purpose it is not worth having! For example the goal may be to discuss a problem that occurred in a manufacturing process that caused major impact. The agenda might include the cause of the problem, contributing factors, and steps that need to be taken to prevent the problem from reoccurring.

Another example could be a sales meeting with a prospective customer. Before the meeting, items to be discussed should be raised with all attendees from the presenting company so that they are aware of how the meeting is intended to progress. Each attendee should be apprised of his or her expected contributions, possible negative reactions by the customer and the responses to those reactions.

A good meeting is usually prefaced by good preparation and forethought. A poor meeting conversely, is usually called with little thought or preparation.

In addition, only persons with input should be asked to attend meetings. It is useless to surround the table with people that have little or no input or reason for being there. Usually, the more people in a meeting, the less effective that it is. Some companies seem to conduct business in a series of meetings, with attendees wandering en masse from one meeting to another. This leaves people with little time to think, plan, and direct. Upper management should set the pattern of holding effective meetings and discourage unnecessary ones.

Meetings should be held to an agenda and they should not be allowed to become a forum for general discussion or heated exchanges. Discussion should be limited and controlled so that no one person monopolises the discussion. All attendees should have a fair opportunity to discuss their viewpoints and reasonings and to present facts.

A good meeting is a pleasure to be a part of as the points of the agenda are discussed, action items are assigned; with a subsequent meeting scheduled to address any issues that remain. It is a pleasure because business is completed and time is not wasted on meaningless meanderings.

QUESTIONNAIRES

These are surveys or questionnaires for information from employees. These may start out as genuine attempts to "poll" company employees to determine their state of morale, their satisfaction, (or dissatisfaction), etc. Some companies even employ outside agencies so that the survey is impartial and the information is not handled by the company.

Most employees have a deep distrust of these surveys as they question how "impartial" the paid contractors would be if real and meaningful comments are made that the company dislikes. The employees often feel that the surveying company might pass information about negative comments to the company, thus endangering their jobs.

Consequently, most surveys are answered with bland, mediocre responses that have little connection to reality. In many cases, employees respond with what they think the company wants to hear. As a result, most surveys are a waste of time and money. As long as peoples' names are attached or there is some way to ascertain who made a comment, there will be little value in surveys.

SUMMARY

Good communications is probably the single most important indicator of a company's openness and willingness to hear positive or negative feedback. Poor communications and hide-bound resistance to change is the most common indicator of a closed and unresponsive company.

To improve communications, trust is vital. When trust is lacking, all communications is suspect. Trust, of course, is more than a buzz-word or an intention, it is a carefully groomed and developed trait that must be developed over time. It comes with the ethical dealing with employees that *is*, and *is seen to be, honest*! One action by the company that is perceived by its employees as unfair or unethical will destroy years of work developing that bond of trust.

In today's environment, the company that communicates well will solve its problems more quickly because it is geared to accept feed-back and use that feed-back to modify its actions and utilise the *best* solutions to its problems. Companies that do not understand and utilise communications properly are handicapping themselves needlessly.

6. TECHNOLOGY

Technology has the possibility of improving the productivity of employees and possible precluding the need for downsizing by allowing employees to do more. It also contains the probability that some of that potential gain will be lost because the technology is applied poorly or because the technology in itself, has factors that lead to lower productivity.

The example of technology downgrading productivity is given in a previous chapter of misusing automated telephone answering services. The intent of introducing such a system is to prevent loss of important calls and to ensure that all calls are responded to quickly. As indicated previously, some employees use the answering service to filter or deflect calls. This certainly decreases productivity. Of course, one never knows how many customers are lost and opportunities are missed because of poor telephone answering discipline. Nor can one define how difficult it is for employees or customers that are trying to conduct business over the telephone when people do not answer their phones or return calls.

I would suggest that all companies using any form of answering system be aware of these problems and take steps to correct them if they want to improve communications, (and business!)

Another example of lower productivity is a long or cumbersome personal computer log-on procedure to one or several of the company's data bases. If the procedure takes five minutes to log-on to an application, and five hundred people have to use the application at least five times per week, at least the equivalent of 5 weeks worth of employee time are wasted per week. Of course, because of security and reality, no-log-on can occur instantaneously, but the log-on time should be kept to an absolute minimum.

Along the same lines, a hidden waste of employee time is poor computer response time. This occurs when an employee is entering data into a central computer, either locally or remotely. After the data for that particular segment or page is entered and the "return" or "enter" key is depressed, there is some time delay while the computer accesses the data and completes the assigned task then displays the next entry or page required. During this time, the employee is unable to do anything.

Some time is required for any transaction to be completed but the time is limited by the speed and size of the computer being accessed, how many other jobs are being accomplished simultaneously, and the number of other people accessing the computer.

The time delay is exacerbated if the data is being entered from a remote location. Added to the delays listed above is the time required to transmit information to the central computer and receive a response.

If you can picture thousands of entries being made in any given day and can imagine each employee pausing while waiting for the computer to respond, you can picture the waste of time involved. Many companies try to monitor response time and take steps to keep it as low as possible. Unfortunately, the answers for solving response time are usually given as larger, faster computers and more storage capacity.

With the advent of servers, a local smaller computer, comes the possibility of reducing response time in a more economic fashion. If the intelligence level of these servers could be increased to the point that they would hold sufficient information and local data bases so that remote locations or specialized departments could complete their work at a local level, response time would be drastically reduced.

Then at some convenient time, the server could automatically hook up to the central computer and at high speed, upload data to update the central computer's database. This way, rather than several hundred users all vying for the central computers' time, perhaps only ten or twenty users would be accessing each server, which would result in a much faster response time. The central computer could access each server on a regular, reoccurring schedule to update central data bases.

This idea has in fact been in use for some time by fast food chains. The central computer automatically calls each restaurant's computer after the close of business each day to determine the money on hand and update central records and deposit that amount electronically to appropriate banks.

Another productivity drain is the medium. Computers contain not only programs to make your employees productive but also programs that are non-productive, such as games and access to the Internet. Standards should be set and explained to employees that define how and when such programs can or should be used. Some companies in fact, already monitor employee access to the Internet. Many of these companies have found that their employees are accessing Internet sites that are clearly inappropriate to company business.

Before the cry is raised of interfering with employee privacy; the employer has given employees access to the Internet for business purposes, not for web surfing. Although web surfing can be interesting and enjoyable during one's own time, only business should be conducted during paid time. Non-business web surfing has the same effect as coming in late for work every day or taking three hour lunches.

Along the same lines is game playing. It is very difficult to determine what employees are doing unless one can randomly views employee computer screens. An employee could appear to be hard at work but instead be busy playing games.

A reasonable approach to both Internet surfing and game playing is to consider what would be appropriate if the information being accessed were printed matter. Certainly no employee would consider opening and perusing a newspaper or magazine during business hours nor would they contemplate playing crossword puzzles. As discussed above, appropriate and inappropriate Internet access and game playing should be discussed with employees and standards set to reduce wasted time.

Another problem that local computer servers might solve is imperfect access to corporation data bases. To be efficient, these data bases must be available constantly so that employees can gather information and enter information. Also these data bases should be designed so that data only should be entered once and that there is no duplication of data gathering.

To define concretely what is necessary, a data base must be secure but quickly and reliably accessible by all valid users. Access, whether local or remote, should be as reliable as a telephone conversation, with no interruptions of access.

As indicated in a previous paragraph, if the local server had the intelligence and data bases to serve a small pool of users, access would be easier and faster. Also, because less levels of technology are involved, it should be more reliable.

Technology, if used correctly has the ability to speed up any corporation's business by intelligent application of these resources. Unfortunately, people that direct these applications often only see their particular sphere of influence and total direction is segmented and falls far short of desired goals that the corporation might have.

Another problem is that computers have the ability to store ever increasing levels of information. Because this is so, companies sometimes are not discriminating enough of the information that they save, and are consequently overwhelmed with information, some of which is vital, much of which is peripheral or even unnecessary.

An example of this would be the records kept on an aircraft. Every action taken by the manufacturer is recorded, every person that works on that aircraft must, and should, log every part used and removed and *any* action taken to support, maintain, or modify that aircraft. Any unusual flight or ground incident should be, and is logged. This is necessary to keep the aircraft flying as safely as possible.

What is less necessary is to determine what the aircraft maintenance technicians do between maintenance or aircraft support actions. This should be the concern of their supervisors. Some companies try to track their employees non-productive time and then management ensures that time is spent in "politically correct" work.

This "spinning" of data to ensure time comes out to some "accepted" norms is not only ridiculous, it is counter-productive as decisions may be based on skewed data.

Each company should start by asking what information do we really need? Then by designing data bases that collect only needed data, one who views this data can make more accurate decisions. Also, any abnormal situations would stand out.

These anomalies could point out training needs, equipment problem areas, difficult or unusual situations, etc., that could be corrected. Information should be graded as vital, necessary, peripherally interesting or unnecessary. Information should not be gathered if it is not acted on or is not used to make decisions.

Yet another cause of technology causing employee inefficiency is the constant upgrade of hardware and software programs. Employees never get to a state of excellence with a given level of software or hardware because, before they get to the point of being totally proficient with a program or piece of hardware, it is up-graded or changed, which drops their efficiency level. A balance must be reached between upgrading new equipment or software and improving employee efficiency.

CONCLUSION

Above are listed some of the ways that technology can steal efficiency from companies. It is probable that many companies wonder where the increased efficiency is that was promised by new technology. After investing much money and effort, often work seems to be just as slow, (or even slower), than before.

7. RE-STRUCTURING

Companies restructure for many reasons, to impress the stock market, to become more competitive or because it seems the thing to do. Sometimes restructuring is necessary to react to changing competitive situations. As noted previously, restructuring of any type is usually counter-productive in that productivity goes down as organizational structures are dismantled and new ones are built. The organizational confusion that is created is accompanied by a sense of employee malaise or inertia. This is because of insecurity, mistrust, fear, or anger. It may be many months before productivity returns to the levels that were attained under the previous organizational structure. If the changes introduced a poor command structure in place of a previous more efficient one, business may never return to the same levels.

Many of the goals of restructuring are valid and would indeed improve productivity. Such goals as "cut down bureaucracy" go straight to the heart of the problem. Corpulent, slovenly bureaucracy prevents the corporation from racing along at full speed. Instead, the corporation plugs along like a car with half the cylinders firing and the brakes dragging. It would be great if bureaucracy could, in fact, be trimmed. Unfortunately, cutting the bureaucracy usually is an action item on an individual's list. An inspired individual may even change some of the more obvious bureaucratic morasses. But the real and actual reduction of bureaucracy cannot take place because of the actions of a few managers. They can't even begin to see or know where wasteful bureaucracy exists unless they enlist the help of their employees. Wasteful bureaucracy hangs from many of the branches of an organization like a snake hangs from a tree, hidden from view to all but the direct users of that branch.

Unfortunately, many corporate efforts, however well intended, tend over time to sink into the clinging mud of inertia and after the early brave attempts and bright catch phrases, these efforts slowly settle out of view as yet another great leap forward turns out to be just another wasted effort.

Pruning these errant bureaucratic log-jams is hard, continuous work that cannot be done without all the employees' assistance. Anyone who thinks otherwise is merely whistling bravely while walking down a dark alley.

For real gains in corporate efficiency, appearance and noise have no place. Many corporate get-well plans are like the circus coming to town; a lot of noise, bright lights and brave pronouncements, only to be followed by the "jaded feeling the day after when the circus leaves." Employees have been there before! They can judge the difference between intent and real action. Companies only kid themselves if they think that employees don't sense from corporate officers' actions and words, and how those intents are put into place at their level, if a program is real or just merely lip service.

Restructuring, if and when necessary, should be carried out in a manner that is logical and can be seen to make sense. You can sell a bill of goods to your employees and they will buy it because they have no choice. However, they will believe it if it makes sense and is necessary.

A large change like restructuring can take place with or without employees' acceptance. In all but the most drastic circumstances, however, companies should strive to gain employees' acceptance. Any change will meet with employee resistance as they fear the impact that change will have upon them. If they understand the change and recognize the need for it and trust the company, they will resist it less and perhaps even accept it.

For example, some time in the past, a large foreign subsidiary of a US company merged with another company. Each company had its strengths of strong and recognized managers. Upper management took time to determine the best people in both companies and, almost without fail, selected the best person for each management position, regardless of previous affiliations. The displaced individuals were given other opportunities within the company that utilized their areas of best abilities.

After the various appointments were announced, employees of both of the old companies quickly realized the fairness involved and the ethical approach taken and quickly accepted the changes and began working for the newly merged company with very positive and trusting attitudes.

The merging of the two companies that had been strong rivals into one stronger, merged company was a success because time was taken to logically assess the situation, fairly evaluate employees' strengths and weaknesses, and then appoint the best individual to each position. Since the whole plan was carried through in such a logical manner and since no one was displaced because of it, the morale of employees quickly recovered from the pre-merge slumps and reached new heights. Also great care was taken to re-assure employees throughout and also to communicate as much information as possible to keep employee confidence at a high level. The success of the merger also re-assured concerned customers as they saw the same or better service than they had previously.

This example flies in the face of "take no prisoners" takeovers that are all too common today. These take place when companies take over or merge with a smaller or less financially powerful company. Pick up any financial paper and you'll read of the layoffs associated with such hostile takeovers. In some cases, a certain amount of trimming is undoubtedly necessary but could be covered by normal attrition such as retirements and elimination of poor performers. **The question one could ask is "if most of the peoples' jobs were justified before the merger, why are they not equally as justifiable after?"** In most cases, they are! In many cases, after a take-over or merger the new company is weaker because of excessive layoffs and the determination to fit "cookie cutter management" to the company that has been taken over without learning about the new business segment. Often this lack of understanding leads to heavy losses of the company that has been taken over until the stronger company finally sells it off to another company.

If internal restructuring must take place, it should result in improved lines of communication, clearer control of profit or loss, and employee acceptance, if it is to be successful. It should be logical and be seen as such by employees. If the restructuring creates confused reporting structures and poor or ineffective decision making processes, it will, of course be less than successful.

8. Fragmentation

Many companies have areas of development, organizations, and departments that often have areas of common interest, knowledge, or information. Unfortunately, because of the tribalization of these different areas, very little cross-feed develops between these groups with resulting duplication of effort and resulting inefficiencies.

Cross-feed from engineers, developers, etc., from previous products can help short cut development of new products. It is necessary to have that feed-through from previous products to prevent the new group from starting from scratch and perhaps heading off in the wrong direction, only to expend time and effort to arrive at the same conclusions that the previous group arrived at earlier.

Fragmentation or compartmentalization also prevents departments from working together smoothly as each department focuses only on what is important to it rather than what is best for the company. This often impedes normal transactions between different departments as one department may make unilateral decisions that adversely affect the users of that department. An example of this would be a parts department setting an arbitrary level of parts without consulting the users of those parts as to the effect that may have on them.

Companies are made up of a various number of different departments with different functions but the common goal of working together toward the common good of the company. Fierce independence of a department is only self-centred egoism that does not serve the company well. A company is like a large jigsaw puzzle. All pieces are necessary to complete a puzzle, just as all departments must work together as a team for the company to be totally successful.

Say, for example, that the sales department in a company is given pre-eminence over other departments. While sales is very important as the salesmen deal directly with customers, the manufacturing department is just as vital, for without their good work, the products would be of poor quality, and hence, unable to be sold..

Also the service department that installs, maintains, or repairs equipment, keeps the customers' good esteem. This makes it easier for salesmen to continue selling successfully.

Every department, from administration to shipping has an equally important role to play. Each must be part of the team and work toward to a common goal for the company to be most successful.

Depending upon the personalities of the managers and employees of the different departments and company politics, different departments can develop a self-centred, self-interest that is detrimental to company success.

This can become so bad that at times some departments become like little enclaves or fiefdoms, with their chief task being protection of their domain. Of course, this creates administrative log-jams because more time is spent by those departments defending their territory than working for the company.

Sometimes the problem is a mindset or perspective that the department has of other departments that causes problems. Distant departments tend to underestimate other department and their workloads. A common statement is often heard, "Oh, they have plenty of time to do that." The affected department may in fact be overworked, short-handed etc.

This tribalization sometimes comes about as a defensive measure against what may be perceived as unfair or unreasonable actions by other department or upper management.

One of the management "fads" of recent memory was the "customer / supplier agreement." This was an agreement that was reached between different departments that discussed what the user wanted and also what the supplier would do to achieve those goals. This idea was often a result of quality programs and was a sound idea. What happened in practice is that much discussion went back and forth, formal agreements were made and posted on walls and then, promptly forgotten. These agreements in most cases did not, or were not allowed to address the working relations between different departments and really solve the problems. In most cases the customer / supplier agreement ended up being yet another well intentioned idea that, after the initial efforts, was quietly forgotten and never given the backing and continuous attention it needed to turn it into a real program.

Consequently, the customer / supplier agreement did little to reduce or eliminate the rampant tribilization that exists between departments in many companies.

Whatever the cause, tribalization is counter-productive and should be addressed when it occurs. Otherwise, it slows the flow of business and prevents the use of new or innovative ideas. No company can be totally successful as long as some degree of tribilization slows the interaction and flow of information, supplies, or service between different departments.

One of the symptoms of tribalization is the "not invented here" syndrome. This means that any idea not generated by a department will not be given consideration since it came from outside. Many ideas that could generate new business opportunities or make work easier are doomed by this mindset.

This resistance to ideas and suggestions from outside may be in part defensive in nature to protect the stature of the department. It may also be egotistical in nature in that employees in that department, because of their education, skills, or position in the company, think that they know best.

An example of this is a development team for a new product. Rather than gathering expertise and wisdom from previous designers of like products, the new team charges off into the wilderness, only to face many problems that had been addressed and solved before.

Some input from previous design teams would help highlight previous problem areas and discuss what was successful and what was not. This crossfeed would help the new design team get out of the starting blocks with a head start and most probably end up with a better design for the product.

Fragmentation also occurs when a department or group unilaterally takes actions or makes decisions that adversely affect other groups or departments. Just as a horse in a team cannot go off in a different direction to the rest of the team, neither should a department make decisions without discussing the impact that those decisions may have on other departments.

What develops when fragmentation is allowed to run unchecked is an ongoing series of small skirmishes between different departments. This can be very detrimental to normal business operations when departments are acting in such a self-centered fashion. Unfortunately it is nearly impossible for upper management to ascertain when departments operate in this manner.

Only the departments that have to utilize the services of a problematic department will be aware that there is even a problem. Of course, as mentioned previously, many companies have contracts of agreement between interacting departments but unfortunately before the ink is dry on many agreements, the contracts are invalidated by employee actions.

Since this is so, one way that better cooperation could be effected between departments is to develop an evaluation system. This system could be a quarterly "report card" on the various facets of service received from all supplier departments. Since only the users of a given service from a department can evaluate the service given by that department, the users should evaluate those services honestly and factually.

Once this feedback is received from all user departments, the serving department manager and his manager could evaluate the feedback and look for problem areas. The feedback may indicate a policy, or a particular segment of a department that is causing a problem. It may also highlight a particular user department that indicates problems. This may indicate a human interaction problem, misunderstood or misapplied policies, etc.

It is important to evaluate the relationships between all users of service and all suppliers of services within a company. These evaluations should not be used as bludgeons to beat a service supplier into line but as tools to understand and improve working relationships.

As every employee is evaluated by his manager or supervisor, so should each department be evaluated by its users. These should be completed on a reoccurring basis. As suggested previously, a quarterly or a semi-annual evaluation would give regular feedback that should improve cooperation between departments and once the initial major problems and policies are worked out, these evaluations should be an indication of efficiency to each department. They should never be allowed to become mere rubber stamp actions by less than energetic managers. This would negate the whole purpose of the evaluation system!

An example of how this could work is given for a manufacturer of home appliances. As an appliance goes through the manufacturing process, each manufacturing technician is both a user and a supplier. He / she is a user because he / she receives the unfinished product from the previous step in the manufacturing process. He / she also receives parts, tools, and other resources so that he / she can do their job. The technicians become suppliers as they pass the product to the next step in the manufacturing process. Of course, quality control technicians try to keep the end quality of the product high by regular checks but the technicians each should have input on the quality and timeliness of the partially assembled product that they receive from the previous step in the assembly line, as well as the parts and resources that they receive from suppliers.

Often the finished product is not the end of the process as the finished product must be shipped, stored, sold and installed by yet other employees.

A suggested way that evaluations could be used is to give high performing departments a bonus that is based on savings generated by low repair costs or rapid service. It may be noted that at the end of the chain, the sales, installation and service technicians have little apparent feedback. However, they must satisfy the customer, who will either buy more products from the company or go elsewhere with their purchases. But even customers should be asked about all their interfaces with the company to find out what the company does well and what it can improve upon.

No company, regardless of how large or apparently secure, can choose to ignore the customer! Without the customer's satisfaction, any company will fail!!

As indicated above, each department must work together to provide a product or service. Each department is a factor in the success of any company and must work as part of the team and not a walled off enclave.

SUMMARY

The keys to eliminating fragmentation between departments is first to place *all* departments at the same level and make *all* departments responsive to input from other departments. No departments should be allowed to ignore the overall good of the company to its singular advantage.

Second, sound communications should be developed to address problems between departments. Many quality problems only address problems internal to departments, whereas many of the most serious problems impacting company efficiency are caused by poor interdepartmental relations.

Also, steps should be taken to provide feedback on previous products so that the historical perspective will aid in new product development.

Finally, the customer-supplier agreement needs to develop into a report card of what is being done well by each department and what needs improvement. By eliminating friction between departments and setting each one toward a common goal, all can become more successful.

9. Mistakes

These are the errors large or small that employees make that cause angry customers, frustrated management and disgruntled coworkers. In today's stressful workplace, tolerance is low for any errors. Employees are expected to come into a job and perform perfectly, regardless of their experience or confidence level. In addition, employees are often given a totally new responsibility and are expected to have full expertise in all aspects of the new responsibility from the start. Of course, perfect performance and perfect employees are non-existent. In the real world, real people make mistakes, some are small and perhaps overlooked. Some are massive, with major impact.

Note, however, that the only way never to make a mistake is to not do any work or take on any new responsibility. *Employees will make mistakes*! They should learn from their mistakes and not make the same mistake again but if they are doing tasks, they will make real and perceived mistakes.

What is a perceived mistake? A perceived mistake is a situation in which the employee does everything right and the situation still goes wrong.

An example of this would be an irate customer situation. It may be that the employee follows correct guidelines, is tactful and listens but the customer still raises the issue with upper management. The customer is always right! Of course that is true. But because of personality differences between the customer and the employee or totally unreasonable demands on the part of the customer, it may be impossible to satisfy irate customers.

Of course, the customer will have to be placated by the manager but when it comes time to evaluate the "mistake", rather than automatically considering that the employee was wrong and the customer was right, consider the employee's viewpoint. Also take into consideration the employee's past customer relations habits and finally, listen to other employees or even customers that may defend the employee. It may have been an impossible situation for any employee to successfully resolve.

If mistakes are a normal part of the job, why discuss them? Mistakes have many causes, some cannot be preventable but others may be. By discussing mistakes, the ones that can be prevented can be addressed, at least preventing future problems that they cause. You can rest assured that the vast majority of employees *do not want to make mistakes*! It is not as though they sit around and think, "what can I mess up today?" All employees that care about their jobs dislike making mistakes as much as management, (and the company), dislike the mistakes.

What Causes Mistakes?
Human Factors

Carelessness - Of course, some errors are caused by carelessness and lack of attention. They can also be caused by lack of confidence and lack of experience. What may be construed as carelessness may just be newness in a job or lack of familiarity with a facet of that job. It is always easy for someone outside a situation to "second guess" and place blame. What may appear to be easy from afar may be confusing and unclear when standing in front of the problem.

So before assigning blame as "pure carelessness," examine the real situation. Very few people take so little pride in a job that they cause problems by being careless.

Tiredness - Of course errors occur when employees are too tired to make decisions at the level required. No one performs at their peak performance if long work hours cause excess tiredness. If the work is complex, demanding, or the work situation is under high stress, employees can become tired much more quickly, causing more problems.

An example of an operator error caused by tiredness would be a truck driver falling asleep at the wheel of his truck, causing an accident. Often it is a combination of factors such as a high priority load, long work day, monotonous road, etc., that exacerbate the tiredness, causing the accident.

Another example could be a computer operator entering the wrong response to a computer console message and causing a job to fail. When a person is tired, their mental acuity is obviously lower. When tiredness is coupled with job stress, errors are more common.

Habit - People are habitual creatures. We continue to do things in the same way even when procedures change. The longer that we develop a particular habit, the harder it is to break.

An example of this would be a pilot flying an airplane with retractable gear. If the pilot was used to moving the landing gear control downward to lower the gear before landing was transferred into a new plane in which the landing gear control moved upward to lower the gear, he / she would probably land with his / her gear up.

Stress - Abnormal stress can cause employees to make errors. Take the same action that they have done repeatedly the correct way and place them in a high stress situation and they can very easily make errors. A good example of this is to have a person walk along a fallen log. Of course, it is easy, but put that same log one hundred feet in the air and suddenly it becomes an impossible task. The only thing that has changed is the stress level because of the seriousness of making a mistake. This is an exaggeration but high stress levels caused by the job, worries about job security, and personal concerns can all lead to increased level of errors.

Using the example above of the pilot of an airplane with retractable gear and place him / her on a flight into a very busy airport and add poor weather conditions and perhaps some minor problems and he / she could land the plane with the gear up.

This has been such a problem that aircraft manufacturers have developed warning systems to detect if the gear is lowered when it should be and to sound very loud alarms when it is not. Even then, pilots have landed gear up with alarms blaring loudly.

Over confidence - Many times mistakes are made because the individual thinks that he / she knows how to do the task, only to be proven wrong when problems occur.

Distractions - Often errors are caused by something distracting the employee's attention to something else. When the employee returns to the task at hand, a step may be missed that may cause major problems.

An extreme example of this type occurred some years ago in an airliner descending to land at an airport in Florida. One of the instruments had a burnt out bulb, which caused the entire crew to become distracted from the task at hand, that of monitoring aircraft altitude, and to become focused on repairing the burnt out bulb. This distraction had a fatal ending as the aircraft crashed into the Everglades, killing many people.

OTHER FACTORS

Lack of knowledge - This is the most common cause of mistakes. This ranges from lack of basic background knowledge to specific knowledge about the task to be accomplished.

An example of the former would be an electrician wiring a house without being aware of the local electrical code requirements and having to rewire certain areas.

An example of the latter would be an auto technician replacing a faulty part with a similar part without realizing that there was a new, much improved part that should have been used.

Poor Design - More than a few mistakes are caused by poor design. Many products are designed with insufficient consideration for how they are used and how they could be misused.

An example would be the connectors on the printed circuit card on the back of a personal computer. If the computer were designed so that the same plugs were used for different components, they could, (and would be), plugged into the wrong places by some person, at some time. This could either cause the PC not to work or could even destroy some of the components. This is the so-called "Murphy's Law." This is a semi-humorous statement that says "if a thing can be done a wrong way, it will." Amazingly, this simple premise of designing things so that they cannot be done wrong is ignored, much to the misfortune of the affected companies.

Another example of poor design is unguarded switches and controls on computer equipment. It is not unusual to have cleaning personnel inadvertently bump a switch with a broom handle, disabling a piece of equipment or perhaps even causing the entire computer room to stop operation.

These problems can be prevented by "goof" testing the equipment. In other words, the question should be asked "what would happen if" and subject the equipment or software to inexperienced poking and prodding to observe what preventive measures should be taken. Often these are "no cost" improvements if done early in the design stage.

For example, the personal computer could be designed with different sized and shaped connectors so that no connectors could be plugged incorrectly. The second example, of the computer equipment with unguarded switches could be designed to have controls behind marked panels or with guards over switches.

Poor Documentation - Many companies suffer from poor, incomplete or incomprehensible instructions. It is not surprising that users and employees make mistakes, it is only surprising that they make as few as they do! Designers of hardware equipment and software program developers often provide poorly defined instructions for the operation and service of their products. This causes countless mistakes that are blamed on the users and service technicians of the equipment.

Good technical writers should be given the leeway to write and test procedures using inexperienced persons to test the correctness and veracity of the written instructions. This would prevent many subsequent disasters that cause customer anguish and cause expensive redesign work.

Standardization - Another cause of mistakes is lack of standardization. An example of lack of standardization is the placement of controls on automobiles. For example, one car had the horn actuator switch located on the end of the turn signal wand. Of course, if one needed the horn in an emergency, one pushed the steering wheel where the horn switch is normally located. It would be much safer if emergency controls were all standardized in location and operation.

Another example of standardization is an aircraft cockpit. The location, shape, and size of controls aids the pilot in selecting the correct control by feel. For example, the landing gear control is usually shaped like a wheel. Other lesser controls are square, triangular or hexagonal shaped rather than just cylindrical, so that the pilot can differentiate between them, preventing potential problems that could be caused by selecting the wrong control.

Overly complex work environments - Another cause of mistakes is the overly complex work environments that are common in many technical areas. Just as the equipment is becoming increasingly simple and more reliable, so is it being tied together in fiendishly more complex systems and networks. Because the systems are so complex, they have evolved beyond the bounds of a single person's expertise.

Because of this complexity, equipment or software products that worked well when tested individually can become erratic and ill-disciplined when fed multiple and overlaid instructions from many different sources or programs. The complexity also lays the trap of simple, supposedly correct actions that cause various problems because of the interactions of the sundry components in a complex network.

Lack of Tolerance - Along with the above reasons for making mistakes goes the lower level of tolerance for any mistake, whatever the cause. This causes unbelievable stress on employees trying to cope with high levels of expectation with less than perfect training, equipment and software.

PREVENTION - HOW CAN MISTAKES BE PREVENTED.

Training - This of course is the best way to prepare any worker for any working environment. If an employee fails to accomplish a task, most often one will find lack of realistic training as a prime cause. If the task is of a highly complex nature, reoccurring training is a necessity to keep employee' knowledge current. Too often, current training provides information about the product or service but too little information about the actual use of the product. The fine details are nice to know but what employees really need to know is how to use it. They need to know the real "nuts and bolts" of doing tasks. For example, "when I see this on my computer screen, what do I do?"

Tiredness - Workload and working conditions may cause tiredness on the job. If excess hours are being worked or multiple responsibilities are being accomplished, employee fatigue will result. Work load must be kept at a reasonable level otherwise errors will occur more often.

Another factor to consider is shift work. Workers take time to adapt to new work-shifts. Constantly changing shifts can cause employees to be continuously tired. If shift work is a necessity, employees should be assigned to a permanent shift at least for a period of months, so that their bodies get used to the changed sleeping and working cycles. Frequent breaks are necessary in out-of-normal shifts or when doing highly complex work. These more frequent breaks will keep employees working at a higher level of efficiency.

Habits - By having standards of procedures that keep reoccurring tasks similar, habit mistakes can be reduced. Companies need to understand that any major change will be accompanied by a higher level of errors. Of course companies must make changes but if they keep the changes incremental rather than massive, their employees will be able to cope with the new changes with fewer errors.

Stress - Whenever possible, keep stress levels as low as possible. Reduce outside factors that cause stress such as worry about job, department dissension, etc. Companies would not operate an important machine with excessive friction on its bearings; they would lubricate the machine so that it ran smoothly. So must companies reduce friction from employees work situations, so that they can work more effectively.

Lack of knowledge - As indicated, good realistic training goes a long way to eliminate lack of knowledge. It is important to provide current information for all tasks that employees will perform. A good example of providing knowledge is "help menus" on personal computers. Never assume that employees remember how to do a given task. It may have been months since they last accomplished the task, it may have changed, or they may be very tired. Cautionary warnings with explanations also help. These are computer menus that warn what will happen if an unusual response that was given is re-entered, and often ask, "Are you sure?"

Poor design - Some steps have been taken by hardware and software designers to design products that help to prevent errors. Much more work needs to be done in this area!

By applying standardization, known successful solutions should be coupled with ergonomically designed products. These products should be designed to eliminate operator errors or repair mistakes. Designs should be made as simple as reasonable with as little potential for errors as possible.

Poor documentation - This is an area that all companies could improve on! Any task should be able to be accomplished by a novice with some form of documentation to guide them in accomplishing any task. It must be assumed that the person was poorly trained, or has not accomplished the task recently or is tired or not feeling well. If documentation is developed to this level, many major mistakes will be prevented.

Lack of standards - As stated previously, if standards are applied to make equipment and software similar where possible, it will help employees gain higher skill levels than if the job environment is constantly changing.

Overly complex work environments - Whenever possible, these should be simplified. Whenever that is not possible, automatic tolerance and recovery to inadvertent actions must be built into equipment design and software control.

SUMMARY

It should be understood that currently tolerance for mistakes in any business is low or non-existent. It should be also understood that hardware equipment and software designers must develop new products that reduce possible mistakes. Finally, it must be understood that management can take steps to reduce errors by providing realistic training and more valid management policies. Finally, developing a good working environment will reduce stress and lower error levels.

10. Labor Changes

The business place is in a state of change just as it has always been since the workplace changed from the cottage industry level to more modern industrial manufacturing. Much of this change has been driven by increased competition. In the past, business as usual was OK., since competition was not so fierce. Since the rapid industrial growth that was caused by the Second World War and continued throughout the period of the cold war, caused healthy finances for all but the most inefficient businesses, many businesses did not make serious attempts to run their businesses effectively. Recently, with the demise of much military spending since the cold war has ceased, and with the advent of global competition, efficient business is not a desire, it is a necessity for survival!

As discussed in other chapters, downsizing is one major step taken by many companies to try to redress the performance of their business. As it is true that a few businesses were overstaffed, in some cases this was a necessary step. In many others, downsizing was not needed as much as a return to more stringent financial controls. In many other cases it was totally wrong.

In the last two instances, what the downsizings have caused is higher workloads to retained employees. This in turn, has led to higher stress levels, longer work hours and less time for family and hobbies. The retained employees are supposed to be grateful that they have a job, even if they don't have time for much of a life outside work.

This flies in the face of the idea of having a well balanced life with work, family, and play, each being equally important. It was not many years ago that workaholics were pitied because they had no life aside from work. Now, because of downsizing many employees have been forced to dedicate a larger portion of their time to work. This, of course, is at the expense of personal and family time.

The increased work load that has been forced on much of the working population will take its toll in increased marital problems and stress related illnesses. It will force many people that will not accept long term overwork to seek other employment.

Once again, one can see that downsizing causes increased workload and is merely a short term expedient that, if continued, must take its toll by decreasing long term success of any company.

JOB CHANGES

Because of technology, many jobs are changing. The old stereotype of going to work at a workplace at a given time, working for a set period and then going home is changing for many. Of course, many jobs in manufacturing, retail, and direct customer service must remain the same but many others have and should change. Many types of businesses are now open twenty four hours per day. Of course some businesses in health and public safety have always worked round the clock but now some retail stores are open twenty four hours per day to service the clientele that are around at all hours. These twenty four hour operations stretch the ability of management to control and interface with shift employees.

One consideration to aid employees that have to work such shift work is to vary shift start times to that employees do not have to fight peak traffic to get to and from work.

As discussed elsewhere, another consideration for companies with shift workers is to realize that it is difficult to adapt to constantly changing shifts. It is better to make shift assignments as a relatively long term assignment, say for three to six months. That way, employees can adapt to the shift work better. Another consideration for work outside normal prime shifts is that employees will need more frequent break periods to remain effective.

TECHNOLOGY CHANGES

Technology has caused other changes, including the way the job is structured. With the advent of the personal computer and its implementation as a tool by some workers, jobs have changed greatly.

When once it was necessary to be physically at the workplace to do one's job, for many companies, it may no longer be necessary. A programmer at home may be able to log-on to his / her computer to determine why a job on the company's mainframe failed, and then to suggest steps to make it run correctly or even make software repairs remotely.

Another example is a salesman. Once it was necessary to spend much of their time in an office because of the secretarial services and communications focus that the office provided. More recently, because of improved communications and laptop PCs and printers, the office can be wherever the salesman may be.

Another example is an appliance service technician. Once he / she may have needed to go by his / her office to look up parts and look through service manuals. Now, many of the companies are developing "online" data bases that provide parts and service manuals via hand-held laptop computers.

What the above implies is that in many cases, the traditional office is no longer a necessity. Of course, the media has presented examples of telecommuters that work from home totally. This will become much more common as companies become more innovative and more realistic.

The hardest thing to overcome to developing into this new style of workplace is management mindset. It will be very difficult for some managers to accept and help develop these changes.

There are some constraints to be weighed before considering telecommuting or other like possibilities. There are some employees personalities that work well under direct supervision but poorly when working on their own. Other employees like the day-to-day interface with other employees for companionship and support. Probably only fifteen or twenty per cent of any given company's employees would be successful if given a telecommuting or other independent job.

It takes a self-reliant and self-disciplined person that is equally at ease in a group or working solitary to work well in a self-sufficient situation. These are the most well-rounded and stable individuals. Many people that work well when under direct peer group pressure may lack self-discipline and perform poorly when working on their own.

The first step to using employees in a more independent environment is to determine the employees that have the skills needed. The next step is to define which employees will work well in a solitary and self-disciplined environment. Only problems will result if employees that need some degree of direction or discipline are allowed to work in a remote situation.

The next step to take when attempting to develop a new working environment is to develop a firm understanding between the employee and management as to what acceptable levels of performance are. Unless a firm understanding is reached on what is expected of the employee and what levels of performance and response to telephone or pager calls is expected, the attempt to set up off-site employees will not work. If the employee is unavailable when an important task needs completing, the company will soon return that employee to an in-company office. Similarly, if performance levels are below expectations, the company will not be satisfied with the telecommuting employee's work.

Notice that this type of work environment changes the concept of work from time on the job to work accomplished. This could be measured by completion of projects, sales calls, or numbers of service calls or visits. In the past, companies have confused putting in time with accomplishing work. The punctuality of the employee arriving and departing work was considered as vital as the work accomplished. With the new working environments, the emphasis must be placed on tasks completed.

This is, for many companies, a new and disconcerting concept. But the completion of tasks has always been vital so that the total job requirements are met.

An example of a group of workers that could just as easily work from home are computer service engineers. A service engineer can now check equipment operation from a remote personal computer. He / she could get up in the morning, and while drinking his / her first cup of coffee, check all the equipment at various customer accounts from the PC. As service engineers are paged if a device on a customer account fails, they are working wherever they are, so long as the pager is available. The important fact is that quick response to any problem or to any need for assistance is necessary.

Of course, customer site visits are necessary to maintain equipment at peak levels by performing preventative maintenance. Another reason site visits are crucial is to develop and continue strong customer relations. These service engineers and many other workers could perform their work from home, responding as needed for various service calls, meetings, etc. The question is not can this be done but should it? This is the decision that companies must make. If it makes economic sense for a company to have some of its employees work from home and it can be done at least as well as working from an office, it should be done.

What many companies will begin to realize that traditional offices are an unnecessary cost that can, in many cases, be supplanted by self-reliant employees working from their own home. With the home computers that many employees have now, combined with the concept of task completion, many employees that now work out of offices could spend much of their time working out of a home office.

The company could provide much smaller, less elaborate workspaces for the occasional visits that employees might make to a central office. Hotel meeting rooms could be used for larger meetings or customer presentations. This way, companies could cut down on expensive office space and only require a fraction of the office space now required. Another reason that companies might consider employees working from home is to redress the balance of work, family, and play. By allowing employees to accomplish some of their work out of their home, companies could reduce the stress caused by daily commuting to a central office. It would also allow employees more time for their family by eliminating at least some of the commuting time.

One major problem with remote employees is the necessity to take steps to keep employees interacting. Occasional employee social or business meetings may be necessary to reinforce company direction and keep morale up. This may be one of the chief concerns of human resource departments as new working environments come into being.

SUMMARY

As discussed above, for many companies and their employees, many different factors have led to changes in the workplace. These changes will continue and will be used by many companies to increase employee effectiveness and reduce costs. These changes will be resisted by many managers and some employees as they will see it as a loss of control or a loss of familiar environment, respectively.

Change is the one constant of business. New ideas, new technology, and competitive pressures all cause changes that must be accommodated by companies and their employees if long term success is desired.

11. RE-ENGINEERING

Once a product is developed and in use, making changes to that product is many times more expensive as correction to the product is before it is in production. Of course, sometimes engineering changes on completed products are necessary for safety or product reliability improvements. The cross-feed from design teams on earlier products that is suggested in an earlier chapter would prevent some of the re-engineering that may otherwise be necessary. Continuity is necessary to take what was successful on older products and blend that with the advancements of the new products. This may also aid in developing a new product that is comparatively *"seamless"* compared to the older product it may be replacing.

Whenever possible, designs should be made so that the product is as easy or easier to use than its predecessor. This will also aid customers by requiring less training to accommodate the new product. This is another strong sales point to customers that already have a preceding product.

At the very least, the cross-feed can help at the nuts, bolts, and component level by defining problems that were encountered and the methods used to surmount them. There is absolutely no point of wasting design time and effort to overcome problems that have been resolved previously.

Another area that companies can address to improve profitability is to keep design changes limited to as early in the life of a new product as possible. Any hardware or software that is designed goes through a series of design stages before the end of the product's life. The cost of these changes can vary greatly, depending on when in the product life-cycle that changes are made.

For example, for changes that are made during the development stages of the product, costs are low. As the design matures and turns into an almost completed product, the costs begin rising, and finally, when the product is in use by the customer, change costs are very high.

An example of the relative costs of changes are: In early development stages on a sliding scale from one to fifty, the relative cost of change might be a one; in an almost completed product, the cost of change is perhaps ten times the cost of change in early development stages; for a product that is in use by the customer, the cost of change can be up to fifty times the cost of change in early design stages.

It is obvious that if companies can reduce the number of product changes later in their products' lives, they can reduce the cost of those products or make more profit. It is impossible to totally eliminate late changes because if a company waits until they have a perfect product, the window of opportunity for selling that product will be lost.

An example of the first stage of change would be the design of a radio. After the design is in place, decisions will have to be made to select components to fulfill the various requirements. Of course, during this stage it is very easy to change from one component to another for a particular function.

The next example would be the same radio but when it is built and being produced. Now a failure of a component will be more costly because the product line must be stopped, a new component must be procured, the old component removed and the new component replaced on all the radios produced thus far.

The last example is the same radio that has been sold in large numbers before a quality or safety problem is detected. Of course, it will cost much more to return the product for repair because a repair facility will have to be set up to replace the faulty component; shipping, handling, and administrative costs will be high because the product must be returned, repaired, and then returned to the customer. In addition, there may be legal costs if a safety problem has caused injury. So it is apparent that it makes sense for companies to limit, wherever possible, late changes in a product's life.

COMPONENTS

For hardware products, one of the most important ways to limit re-engineering costs is by selection of quality components.

To put this in prospective, unless a company deals in raw materials, they deal with components, either manufactured in-house or supplied from an outside source.

An example of this is the average car. The steel that comes from outside suppliers is turned into the body, frame, and major components, such as the engine, transmission, etc. Most of the remainder of the car, the various motors, brakes, switches, lights, sensors etc., comes from outside suppliers.

Often the cause of expensive recalls are components that are built outside of specified tolerances, or are of lower than acceptable quality. It does not matter if the cause of problems with safety or quality is a two dollar component, the damage done to a company's cash-flow is great. This is exceeded only by the intangible cost of lost customer confidence in the product.

Consequently, it is very important to ensure that supplied components are of sufficient quality to do the job they are designed for and also that all components that are received from the supplier meet these specifications. In fact, one of the most critical tasks that a company can do to insure high product quality is to verify that the same high quality of suppliers' goods that was originally ordered, constantly flows from the component suppliers. Quality inspectors must verify that the quality of goods received meets or exceeds the expected standards. Once good quality supplied goods are received, it is then the responsibility of the manufacturing line technicians and quality inspectors to verify that the finished goods meet the standards of quality set by the company.

Component quality is vital to a product's success. A customer may buy one product from a company but if less than satisfied with overall quality, they will not buy another.

This is one of the reasons that Japanese manufacturers have made such inroads in the automobile and home electronics market places. For example, they have taken the lead that they gained in inexpensive compact cars and used that reputation of quality to develop mid-range and luxury cars with the same high reputation for quality. Quality and reputation are what aids sales efforts and make selling new products to existing customers much easier. Good quality products also reduce after sales problems and costs by lowering the need to repair or replace faulty products or components.

CUSTOMER ADVISORY BOARDS

Just as improving component quality will reduce the amount of re-engineering necessary, so will the use of customer advisory boards.

Rather than designing a product and then having to change it because it does not meet customer requirements, it would be better to find out what the customer wants and needs before starting the design cycle.

A company will have to spend some money to involve its customers in the design of a new product but it will be money well spent. It would be pointless to spend millions of dollars to develop a product that when manufactured, cannot be sold. It would be much better to find out what the customers need and even let them help set some of the requirements for the new product.

An example of how this could be done is for a car manufacturer to offer a free service to the owners' of cars. Customers could be picked with cars at various stages in the product life. For example, customers could be selected with cars with thirty thousand miles of usage, sixty thousand etc. These customers could then be surveyed to find what was successful about the cars and what problem areas they had discovered. This way, problems could be detected and designed around in new products.

HISTORY

Another tool that could be used to lower re-engineering costs is to analyze component failures on existing products and determine what components, (and suppliers) performed well or poorly and use this to make decisions for components on similar new products.

Of course, totally new products may have no direct correlation to previous products but certainly past history should provide reliable suppliers of components.

SURVEY

Another way to evaluate existing products is to survey technicians for problem areas. For example, an automobile service department may find that a simple task such as changing an oil filter may take two or three times longer than it should. This will drive up the cost to the customer as well as increasing the workload on the service department. This information can be passed back to the design department so that it can be rectified in future models.

An example of just such change occurred some years back on a newly developed military aircraft. When the prototype aircraft was completed, the chief design engineer gathered all the systems design engineers together and asked them if they had any changes that they needed to make before declaring the aircraft ready for test by the military. All the designers shook their heads. The chief design engineer then asked them all to take the aircraft to Alaska and operate it in the same conditions that service personnel would have to when the aircraft became fully operational.

At the end of the month, many of the designers made modifications to their systems to make them more maintainable. In this instance, the design engineers that acted as service technicians while the aircraft was being tested under difficult and demanding environments provided their own feedback.

STANDARDIZATION

Once a good supplier for a particular product is found, sufficient quantities of that product should be planned so that no costly product mid-life changes to another component becomes necessary. Often a newly introduced component can cause some undesirable traits in the product because of some unforeseen differences between the old and new components. Then, in addition to the extra amount that the new component may cost to purchase, more money may also have to be spent re-engineering the product to address these shortcomings.

SUMMARY

The suggestions above will reduce the level of re-engineering to as low a level as possible. In addition, if the various steps are taken before the beginning of a design of a new product, little or no extra time should be expended during the design cycle to implement the ideas that the various steps suggest.

12. LOOKING AFTER THE CUSTOMER

While the above chapters suggest steps that can be taken to improve the financial outlooks of companies, there is one vitally important task that must be taken before, during and after the other steps. That step is look after the customer! No company is ever so large that they can ignore their customers or take them for granted. Any other steps that are taken to improve the company are minor in importance compared to looking after the customer!

In this competitive era, there are those that grumble "we treat our customers too well"! A company can never treat its customers too well! Any changes that a company makes that reduces the level of service to customers will lead to customer migration to other suppliers or vendors, and less market share for the unwise company.

Companies downsize because they think that the stock market will applaud their efforts, (which it may). However, when the press reports a company downsizing, that company's customers are sure to wonder if their level of support will decrease because of the reduced number of staff. This is particularly true if they are not totally happy with the current level of support. It is important that not even the perception of decreased service occurs, let alone the reality of actual lower service levels. It cannot be stressed enough how very important real and perceived service levels are.

An example of this occurred when a large computer company went into Chapter Eleven bankruptcy. Of course the company's customers were very worried about their equipment that they had bought or leased from the company. Was it worthless, could they get it repaired, etc.? Of course competitors of the bankrupt company added to the nervousness of the customers by spreading rumours which implied that the company was finished. Some of the more nervous customers changed companies at this time and many others were ready to change.

At this time, the company in bankruptcy considered how vital the existing links with their customers were and took steps to ensure that these links remained strong while the company tried to work out plans to recover.

All direct links with the customer such as sales, service technicians, parts supplies, etc., were untouched while the overstaffed internal administrative areas were reduced. As customer support was maintained at the same or improved levels than previously had been the case, the customers' nervousness declined and they developed a "wait and see" attitude. During this time, the revenue generated by the field force, particularly the service organization, provided much needed capital to re-establish the company's credibility.

Within several years, the company had fought its way back to financial soundness, won back many of the customers that had scattered like lost sheep, and developed new products that assured its future success. The story would have been different if maintaining customer confidence had been ignored.

LISTEN

Make sure that your company listens to your customers. Regardless of what service or product that your company supplies, rest assured that there are competitors that will do everything they can to get your business. Be it on product quality, technological advantage or price, customer input must be taken seriously!

It is important to even involve customers in the development of new products. With customers' input and advice, new products can be crafted that more closely address their needs and wants.

No company can ever sit on its laurels and consider that it has the market cornered on a particular product or service. Competitors will

Downsizing - What it is and What Steps ...

quickly prove how wrong they are. The desire to make ever increasing profits from a good product must be tempered by the realization that customers' ability to pay is limited. Push the customers too hard and they will be driven to the competition!

A good example of this happened to a very large, well respected corporation. For many years, this company had set the direction of many of its customers. If the customer wanted to make a move in a new direction, it was told when, how, and how much it would cost. The large company developed almost into a monopoly because it set the directions of the market place.

Over time, the employees of the company became almost arrogant in their attitudes. The customers were told in some instances, "take it or leave it."

Of course customers began developing resentment towards this company even though the company was providing solutions to their problems.

Finally, after many years, new companies with new products came forth that began to break the stranglehold that the large company had on the marketplace. Customers deserted in droves, and flocked to the new companies, not totally because the new companies had better products but because the customers' resentment toward the large, arrogant company had grown to the point that they were ready for a change.

After many massive culture shocks and readjustments, the now smaller but wiser company pursues better customer relations than in the past.

LEVELS OF SERVICE

The sales and service of companies are typically the "hard shell" of the company that comes in direct contact with the customer. It goes without saying that this must remain strong to keep existing customers happy and provide a base for company expansion and growth.

If used intelligently to feed information back to company management, this "hard shell" can also provide valuable information on customers problems or concerns. This can supplement any direct customer input and should be used to react to problems before they become too large. In many cases, this intelligence will give the company the chance, not only to become aware of a minor problem but also to take steps to resolve it before it becomes a big problem.

One of the main tasks of employees that directly interface with the customer is to develop and maintain good customer relations. The jobs of selling products, maintaining products, etc., are important but developing good customer relations is vital. Without good customer relations, the best salesman with the best product will fail!

Soft Interior

What often forgotten is the soft "interior" of the company. Increasingly this area is being accessed by customers for administrative assistance, technical solutions, software assistance, etc. Companies often fail to realize how frustrating that navigating these internal areas is for customers and just how quickly that positive first impressions of the company are ruined by the frustrating attempt to overcome the inertia of a company's internal departments.

An example would be the telephone answering system. If your customer must hold or listen to a disembodied mechanical voice with level after level of "push one for a real person" or "all our customer service representatives are busy, please leave your name and number and your call will be returned by the next available person," they will be less than impressed. Is this the impression that a company wants its customers to get of their company? If you were that customer, would you stay on the phone or would you hang up and call a competitor?

What these answering systems are saying is: "Mr. Customer, you are not important enough to talk to a real person." "We are too busy to take your trivial problems seriously."

Couple the implied rudeness of a telephone answering system with perhaps an internal department that does not understand the urgency of the customer's problem and it is easy to see how customer dissatisfaction can grow when interfacing with internal departments of a company.

It is common for in-house departments of a company to have less of an understanding of the impact that problems with a product or service may have on a customer. The relatively sedate pace that may be acceptable and desirable in a new product development lab is worlds apart from "its broke and I can't do the job that I bought it for and my boss is really putting pressure on me," environment of the typical business.

Any department that deals directly with customers must be trained to understand these pressures. It would be wise to staff the department with at least some employees with direct experience of customer problems. That way when a customer calls in with a problem, it will be dealt with quickly and properly.

It goes without saying that any employees that deal with customers should have training in customer relations skills as well as telephone skills. It would be a shame to have a good field force with excellent customer rapport undermined by a few rude or inconsiderate internal employees.

WHATEVER'S FAIR

It is important not to drive existing customers into competitors' arms by overpricing products or service. A very close watch should be kept of customer departures. Sometimes the customer may indicate why they have changed vendors but often they just "vote with their feet" and leave. Often customers will not address the real reasons that they leave a company and go to another. Only the customers that seek confrontation will address the real reason for their departure, be it product performance, price, salesman's attitude, poor service, lack of parts, etc. Customers may latch on to some convenient point such as equipment performance to justify their departure. Unless equipment performance has been an ongoing problem that has already brought to upper management's attention, it is not probable that performance is the real issue. A last minute discovery of a performance problem is more often an excuse so that the real issue does not have to be addressed. Customers just reach a point that they no longer wish to continue in the same business relationship and want to find another company that can provide what they perceive is missing.

If an increasing percentage of business is leaving to the competition, a hard and realistic view must be taken at company policies to see if recent pricing or other actions may have caused the departures.

No existing business should be given away unless it is a corporate decision not to compete in a particular market place. When an existing customer goes away not only is existing business lost but also the potential for all future business. Satisfied customers don't leave!

Summary

Of all the suggestions made in this section, none is more important than keeping customers satisfied. No vacuum exists in the business world; if we fail to provide quality products and service at a price that is reasonable, a competitor will detect our failures and satisfy that need.

13. CONCLUSION

This section has discussed some of the aspects of downsizing and its impact. It has also considered some steps that could be taken instead of downsizing to improve cash flow and to make a company more competitive.

It seems that the larger and more impersonal a company becomes, the more that inefficiencies creep in to impede the smooth flow of business. It takes a very focused management structure to trim these causes of inefficiencies. It is more important to reduce these inefficiencies rather than to trim jobs because often what remains after a downsizing is the same inefficient company but with fewer people to cope with the increased workload.

But, of course, any management structure, regardless of its focus, cannot alone remove inefficiencies. Unless management engages the help of its employees, it will not even be aware that these inefficiencies exist.

So the key to making a company more successful is employee involvement. This is not just a buzz-word or concept, to be successful, employee involvement must be a real and long term commitment.

To have that commitment, companies must stop the self-destructive act of downsizing and redevelop the bond of trust that once existed between the company and its employees. An employee cannot or will not give this type of commitment if he or she has fears about the stability of their job. Employee morale must be rebuilt so that the potential that employees have can be nurtured and brought forth.

All companies can be better than they are today! In the process of building a stronger, more competitive company, a strange thing may happen. Employees may regain the respect and trust that they once had for the company and regain the pride that one was part of many companies' culture.

PART 2

HOW TO USE THE "HUMAN" RESOURCE AS THE VALUABLE ASSET THAT IT IS!

14. Introduction

The previous section of the book dealt with steps that companies could take to improve cash flow and efficiency by optimizing some of the factors that typically cause problems. Some of the items discussed are small but their impact far outreaches their size. Some of the items discussed are invisible, while others are obvious. Be that as it may, these factors collectively steal money from the bottom line of a company as surely as an embezzler!

The remaining section of the book deals with using the *"Human Resource."* This asset has been largely ignored in the ever increasing drive to increase short term profits. This drive has lead many companies astray with its alluring promise of better competitiveness or more profit. All too often, it has been a false promise as many actions that have been taken have had negative impacts on the long term viability's of companies. Many of these short term gains have been bought at the expense of employee jobs.

It is though current managers give their human resources as little consideration as they would a machine working on the production line. Perhaps, that should be less than they would the machine, because at least a machine would be serviced and repaired so it could work at its full efficiency.

What companies need to do is to consider the *"human machinery"* and figure out how it can be used better. This consideration would lead to vast changes in the way employees are treated. The actions of the last decade have made the human resources increasingly insecure and unhappy in their jobs. Not only are they overworked in many cases but unappreciated by an aloof and uncaring management structure.

Intelligent companies will realize that they have gone far enough in alienating employees. Once some of the more forward-thinking companies begin to take steps to make employees part of the company family rather than unwanted step-children, their employees will respond by rewarding those companies with increased efforts. As these companies begin reaping the rewards of better employee relations, other less innovative companies will begin to follow the lead of these business leaders.

If some of the ideas suggested in the next chapters are put into place by these forward-thinking companies, they will begin to reap real benefits from their employees. This will not only benefit the company, it will also provide employees with a much more stable working environment and utilize their talents and skills more fully.

As indicated in the chapters below, other companies have used their human resources very effectively in the past and it has led to long term stability and profitability of those companies.

The companies that learn this lesson will prosper and surpass the less astute companies that have not learned to use their human resource. The disenchanted employees of the latter will leave to go to companies that have become better places to work, displaying the same disloyalty to the previous company as it has to its employees.

The future is more than new ideas, new machines, new technology. It is about using the *"Human Resource"* that is the only real continuing asset that a company has.

15. Using the "Human" Resource

Using the "Human" Resource. As indicated previously, the current environment of many companies is in a confused and fearful state. The current fad of downsizing or re-structuring to satisfy a short term advantage on the stock market or to trim overstaffed workplaces has led to unhappy and fearful employees as they see upper management make decisions that do not seem to be in the best interests of the employees, the company, or its customers.

In the future, downsizing will be viewed as a poor management tactic as it eliminates good workers and requires that remaining workers work longer, harder hours. It also creates confusion and decreases efficiency as key employees are eliminated. Another major impact that downsizing has on the workforce is to create insecurity and low morale.

As everyone is probably aware, stress can cause a higher incidence of health problems and family problems. The added stress of longer work hours and higher demands on one's time will certainly result in more health or family problems in the future. Enlightened companies know this and understand that the best plan for their future is to provide staffing levels that are reasonable and economically sound and that allow their employees to have time for a family and personal life.

Of course, added to the causes of stress listed above is the constant nagging concern about one's job. Employees that are over-stressed and worried about their jobs are not going to be as efficient and certainly not as innovative as employees that are less stressed and that have trust in their companies.

As companies look beyond the possible short term gains of cost-cutting layoffs, they will recognise that the top companies in stockholder returns have achieved their status by growth and improved performance, not layoffs. Hence, in the future, cost-cutting layoffs will be recognised as a short term idea played by companies whose management is bereft of good long term solutions.

The sooner that this is recognised, the better, because many companies have in recent years been ignoring the single most important asset that they have: *That is their employees*!

For many years there have been programs that have stressed how to deal with employees; the "***Dale Carnegie*** Course" being one of the prime ones. These have all maintained that the ability to develop a good relationship with employees and help them develop is important. Corporate America has chosen to give these programs lip-service but if recent corporate activity is an example, they have largely ignored the lessons of previous successful managers and companies. The idea seems to be: This is the Nineties, things are different now.

Things are different: Customers are more demanding, competitors snap at our heels everywhere, global competition is a fact of life. In this environment, a company must use all its assets wisely, including its people.

But people are not machines! You cannot use a person when it is convenient and then discard them when it appears they are not needed. People have feelings, they also have dreams and aspirations. You do not have the right to deprive them of those for mere economic advantage.

What is needed is a total rethinking about the importance of the values that our employees bring to the company and how we can utilize these values and use them to the mutual advantage of both the company and the employee.

Another thing that needs to be rethought is the way that a company uses its employees. Although the competition is more fierce and many companies are trying to adapt to rapid technological and social changes, the area that has stood still most or regressed is the way that companies treat their employees.

Although we have advanced in many ways in more fair hiring

practises, we have gone backwards in so far as treating the employee / company relationship as a valued asset. In fact, many companies act as though employees are no more than necessary evils, to be held at arms length and dismissed without any real consideration of the impact that it has on them.

The companies that do not treat their employees as the assets that they are undermine one of the most potent forces at their command: That of the good morale and loyalty of their employees! By just using predetermined, and in some cases, invalid guidelines, companies are turning away or holding down talents that may be the key to their long term success.

CURRENT

Today's average corporation is for most, a depressing and stultifying place to work. Employees are placed in their job and progress lock-step in a very circumscribed area that their job description defines. Many companies dislike innovation and reward suggestions and ideas with resentment in many cases. The status quo is encouraged and any free thinkers are quickly stifled. It seems that the larger the corporation becomes, the less that it listens to or considers its employees and the more regimented that it becomes.

As indicated in other chapters, many companies have become so focused on valuing everything within the company as a profit or expense, that they have lost touch with the ability of using the human resource correctly.

Of course, companies are in business to make a profit! But every business has a cost of doing business. When the company reaches the point of pushing economics beyond the point of reason, they begin imposing upon the goodwill of employees. Once this area of economies is reached, each further reduction in expenses is purchased at the cost of reduced employee morale.

Management has often been so focused on short term financial results, that long term employee morale and corporate financial results are not considered. Below is a chart that defines a hypothetical example of the relative costs of having employees travel to a meeting at head office. It can be seen that the cost of having employees drive to a distant central office is considerably more if one considers the value of their time which is wasted when traveling by car.

Expense	Car	Air
Travel	$57.00	$460.00
Hotel	2 nights @ $75.00 = $150.00	1 nights @ $75.00 = $75.00
Travel Hours	16 hours @ $30.00 = $480.00	4 hours @ $30.00 = $120.00
Meals	9 meals @ $15.00 = $135.00	4 meals @ $15.00 = $60.00
Total	822.00	$715.00

Of course a decision like this depends if a company wants to pay its employees to drive or to think! Necessary travel is a necessary expense of doing business. Of course, if the trip is not really necessary, it is too expensive, however one travels. This is the question that should be asked rather than whether to travel by car or airline; "is the trip really necessary and will it benefit the company?"

The sometimes convoluted financial rationalization that has become a major factor of many companies has taken many of the decisions out of the realm of management and placed them in the financial department. Of course, making a profit is important! It is the only reason that companies exist! But the focus has gone so far that management has lost control of much of the decision making. Consequently many decisions are made that negatively impact employees, to the long term detriment of the company.

In other chapters, steps are suggested to turn this situation around and make employees part of the company again rather than just workers. Once the human resource is treated as a valuable part of the company team, it can be used to help make the company more successful and a better place to work.

The way that employees can do this is by making improvements in products, services, and improving relations between departments. Before the idea that company suggestion programs exist today that can do that surfaces, let us realize that for the most part, the suggestion programs that currently exist are largely sterile with little impact on anything. The reason that this is so is that the head of any quality program is now effectively in a company backwater, far away from the mainstream of production and sales.

Some years back, quality programs were the current fad of the corporate world. During that time, because many companies were striving for ISO 9000 certification, companies paid much attention to quality. Some good work was done to improve product quality but now it is rare to hear the word or idea mentioned.

Of course it was important for companies to become ISO 9000 qualified but there is a higher court than ISO 9000 certification. That is the acceptance and long term satisfaction of the customer. Quality is not a short term fad that can be visited now and again when emphasis once again returns to it. To be successful, quality should be pursued continuously if a company is serious about providing its customers with quality products. Quality should not be a program, it should be a mindset!

To make a suggestion or quality program work, a very strong and well respected manager should be selected to run it. This manager should answer directly to the chief executive officer and have his backing. This is necessary for many of the problems lie deep within mainstream operations. Without CEO support, these suggestions will be met by cold responses from the managers of the addressed problem areas and will cause few real changes.

This is why quality programs have not been as successful as they should have been in the past. First, these programs have not been allowed to cross departmental lines. Many of the most daunting problems within a company lie outside of departments and deal with interaction between departments.

Secondly, in the past, the quality manager has not been given the authority to address these problems if they resided outside a closely circumscribed area. Consequently, many problems stayed hidden, eating like cancers on the profits of companies.

To be successful, the quality manager should have access to all employees and should solicit potential problems and solutions from them. Once a potential problem is defined by an employee, consensus should be sought from other employees. If other employers feel that the problem indeed exists, steps can be taken to redress or improve it. Many of the most troubling and dollar devouring problems may be invisible to upper management. Only with employee's assistance can these problems be brought to light and resolved.

The internal workings of a company often hide departments that cause log-jams in the flow of business. These problems may be caused by policies, procedures, or personalities. Whatever the cause, the objective should be the elimination of these problems and of friction between departments.

How can this help business? Perhaps it could result in a five per cent increase in sales, a five per cent reduction in expenses, or a five per cent shorter response cycle from manufacturing to sale. Many companies would be very pleased with such a cost-effective improvement. But this improvement cannot happen without the assistance of the employees! They know where the log-jams are because they deal with them on a regular basis.

Another facet to using motivated employees is as extra-numary sales intelligence. The average company may have many people that interface with customers and gain what could be important information. If there were a means to gather this information and pass it forward so that it could be acted upon, it could mean increased sales, reaction to potential problems or heading off of competitive inroads.

Along other lines, it has been an increasing trend to hire talent from outside companies rather than using and growing internal talent. This is faulty for several reasons. Sometimes these "hired guns" shoot themselves, (and the company), in the foot because they do not understand the company's business and the relative import of diverse factors. What is lost by bringing in outside help, either to fill positions or as contractor assistance, is the intimate personal knowledge that long time employees would have. These outsiders do not know the company's business and furthermore, in many cases, do not care! In addition, hiring from outside rather than promoting from within sends a clear negative message to aspiring employees.

Another trend with mixed results is the use of consultants. Companies get into major problems and then they bring in expensive, and in many cases, ineffective consultants to help resolve the problems. The reason that consultants are often ineffective is again that they lack the detailed knowledge of the business that is necessary to resolve problems successfully and, in some cases, they lack the motivation that employees that have the long term interest of the company in mind would have.

In many cases, companies have been ignoring the very asset that could help resolve problems and that has the detailed knowledge necessary: That asset is their employees! In many cases management has even chosen to ignore the suggestions from their employees while listening enthralled to similar suggestions made by highly paid consultants. Ask yourself, "which person has the most at stake in the company, a consultant who can easily go to another company, or an employee who has invested much time and effort and will lose his / her job if the company fails?"

In addition to solving interdepartmental problems and providing sales intelligence, motivated employees can also suggest improvements to products and services, making the company even more competitive. As indicated in following chapters, there are many innovative ways to use employees talent that will benefit both the company and employees.

An example of the current financial over-focus on small details and the problems that it causes are the problems of XWZ banking company. The bank does a large amount of printing of customer statements, checks, income tax statements, etc. The company had traditionally used a relatively heavy paper which was more expensive than some lighter weight paper. Of course, because of the amount of printing done in the course of a year, if the lighter paper were used, this would have the potential of saving several hundred thousand dollars per year for the bank. After some strong and heated discussions between the printer operators and the new facilities resources manager, the new lighter weight paper was purchased and put into use.

Suddenly the printer operations department began having major problems. The lighter weight paper began jamming in the printers, causing many print job halts and restarts as the printer operators had to remove the jams and restart the jobs. Even when the paper went all the way through the printers without jamming, instead of folding neatly onto a pile, the paper created horrendous masses of twisted piles of paper. Of course, because of all the jams, much of the lightweight paper had to be discarded. The new paper also caused more printer equipment failures.

Before the use of the new paper, operators could start one printer then go to another printer and start it, etc. Now, operators had to constantly clear jams. The problem got so bad that the printer operations manager had to hire part-time help just to keep the work flowing. Not only that, the delays began impacting the customers, who complained that their reports were late, which was delaying other work.

The printer operations manager blamed the employees that operated the printers until one of the operators showed the manager the difference between the old heavier, but more reliable paper and the newer, less expensive but more troublesome paper. After a few tests to verify that the lighter paper was, in fact, the cause of the problem; the lightweight paper was sent back to the suppliers and the heavier weight paper was again put into use.

The above is an example of short term savings that was not successful because insufficient investigation was not made into the overall impact that it would have. If management had listened to the printer operators when the subject was first brought up and had run tests to see if the new paper was acceptable before putting it into wide-spread use, the major impact that introducing the new paper caused could have been prevented. In the end, the change to the new, lightweight paper cost more than it saved.

How many of these situations are out there costing money and wasting time that are just being dealt with by disgruntled employees because they are not comfortable with suggesting improvements? Too many, I would surmise! Often the suggestions may fall on the deaf ears of managers, who are themselves fearful of rocking the boat by suggesting change.

The above problem is an example of an interdepartmental problem that could be solved by a good quality program with employee backing. The quality manager would need the staff to do a sound investigation of problems and come up with a proposed solution or verify suggested solutions. The quality manager could then present the problem and its solution to the appropriate manager for correction. This is just a beginning of using the human resource. Subsequent chapters look at (new) or different ways of using employees more innovatively. The word new in the previous sentence is in parentheses because these ideas have been used before by innovative companies to improve company performance and make the workplace a more fulfilling setting for the employee.

Many of the ideas were used by Eddie Rickenbacker as he directed Eastern Airways through twenty five successful business years. He did not go for the short term solutions. He wanted to make the company successful for the long haul and he knew that he had to have the employees' assistance to do so. During the years that he was general manager, Eastern Airlines grew and prospered because the employees trusted and believed in their general manager.

Not using the human resource properly is like having a powerful car but just driving it in first gear! Get the employees motivated again and start pulling ahead of the competition.

16. SET THE EMPLOYEES FREE

The environment that exists today in most companies stifles the most valuable asset that those companies possess, that asset is, of course, the *Human Resource*. A reply to this may be "in our company, employees are all happy in their jobs, thank you"! That may be true but just in case it is not, let's look at that statement in more detail.

The environment in many companies is today in a fearful and stressful state. The turmoil created by restructuring, downsizing, belt-tightening, etc., has created a very unhappy work place where employees worry more about their jobs and making missteps that can place them in a negative highlight than they are about doing their jobs well and the success of the company.

In-fighting between departments often takes place when something goes wrong and everyone scrambles to try to deflect the responsibility for the problem somewhere else. Management at lower levels is just as fearful as the workers are about job security and consequently take little interest in making innovative suggestions or realistically addressing on-going problems.

What exists in many companies can be called "trench warfare." It can be called that because it resembles the western front of Europe during the First World War. Every employee wonders if the next bullet has his / her name on it in the guise of a lay-off notice. Consequently, employees mentally retreat to the trenches by remaining as low key and invisible as possible. Many employees have learned from past experience not to take a strong stand on any issue if they value their jobs. Innovation and new ideas are not put forth, not welcomed, and if not discouraged, certainly not encouraged.

In the average company fear and distrust is rampant between different departments, different functions; and between employees and management. This fear and distrust has been sown by past actions of management and misconceived policies. These actions and policies have gradually worn away the trust and goodwill of the employees until every action is greeted with suspicion and concern.

For example, employees sense the unfairness involved when good long term employees are laid off. By this action, the company is stating that the company cares more about possibly saving a small amount of money than it does about being fair to its employees.

In some cases, suspicion even arises that companies may have some deeply hidden ulterior motive, such as laying off senior employees with considerable time and experience and who draw relatively high salaries so that they can be replaced some time in the future with new hires at the bottom of the pay scale.

Of course employees have opinions when poor workers are fired. The attitude of employees is often one of relief, particularly if the other employees have had to do the work of the sub-standard employee and cover for him / her. Often the attitude may be "its about time the company fired employee x." "He / she has not been doing his job since he / she was hired." So the difference is if the lay-off is perceived to be justified, as in the case of the poorly performing employee, or unjustified, such as in the case of the unfair dismissal. The former is accepted as appropriate, whereas the latter is greeting with disbelief, anger, and deep-seated loss of trust.

But returning to the trench warfare concept, once employees perceive that companies are laying off workers in what could be considered an unfair way, the remaining employees will become very careful. They will do exactly what their job description describes, no more or no less. They will not make suggestions or comments to attempt to improve inefficient operations because often innovators, (noise-makers), are the first singled out when a downsizing occurs.

Rather than most companies understanding that people who care enough to comment or make suggestions are valuable to the company's well-being, instead these very people are singled out as troublesome and either muzzled or eliminated.

So warranted or not, many companies have created a situation where their employees work in with a background of gnawing concern about their job.

CHANGE THE ENVIRONMENT

The first step that companies must make is to change the environment. That is a simple statement but making it happen is complex beyond belief. Employees judge their company by its actions, policies and procedures. To change the environment means more than just making a statement that there will be no more downsizing.

A good starting point would to make a change in corporate policy that would state that downsizing is no longer a policy to be utilized unless the company is in or near bankruptcy. It should be also stated that all employee overstaff situations will be resolved by internal transfers or normal attrition such as retirement or employees leaving for personal reasons. Even substandard performance should be addressed by allowing those individuals a reasonable time to find another position.

While addressing policies, it would be a good idea to redress areas that have lowered employee morale. These, in themselves, may be small but combined with other actions that the company has taken, may be the source of unhappy and disgruntled employees. These policies are often made in the guise of saving money but the small savings that these minor irritants gain certainly is greatly offset by the irritation and lowered morale that they cause.

This is merely the beginning! The changes of policy must be followed by real changes in the way that the corporations deal with their employees. Employees have heard so many bold plans and new ideas that have failed with the passing of time that they have become cynical when faced with yet another new plan. Only when the changes are perceived as real, will the employees begin to believe that things have changed.

DEVELOP TRUST

Understand that to get value from the human resource, the company must work to regain the trust of employees. Workers are much more astute than they are credited to be. They will recognize a real change just as quickly as they will sense a "going through the motions" plan. What employees will recognize is a real, long term change in the way that the company perceives and treats its employees. Rather than the confrontational situation that exists today, companies must develop an environment that generates employee trust.

Management can do this by treating employees as they would like to treated if the situation were reversed and they were the employees, and the employees, management. Management must find high ground and look for the "most fair" way to consider new policies and review old policies. It is appropriate to review all actions taken by the company in recent years. Of course, some decisions cannot be unmade but by reviewing past actions in the light of what probable effect that these actions have had upon employees, a perspective can be gained of probable employee attitude. This overview can also enable the company to focus its direction in such a way that the impact on employees is considered before making any future policy changes.

One step that could be taken is to make seniority in a company important again. Time and experience with the company should imply a level of respect and also should imply an increased degree of job security than is presently the case.

Perhaps rather than companies just unilaterally setting up a new working environment, it might prove more successful to involve employees, so that working as a team, employees and management could together come up with plans that would create a better environment.

REDEVELOP THE COMPANY FAMILY

Corny as it may sound, what is missing in many companies is that lack of care that used to be part of smaller companies and intelligent larger ones.

Like it or not, the work relationship is like any other relationship. The longer the relationship exists, the more that both management and employees have invested in it. This investment is both mental and actual. In terms of management, they have invested training, salary, etc., to grow an employee to a more prolific person. Employees have invested effort and time, often to the sacrifice of their family time, to meet the needs of the company.

Rather than ignoring the fact that this relationship exists and that it is important, as many companies do at present, it should be recognized and nurtured.

All human beings have the need to belong, to be a part of something, to have some worth in life. For many, that something is a job! Many people, correctly or incorrectly, identify with, and gain satisfaction from, their jobs. Since this is such a basic need, it would seem reasonable that astute companies would encourage it rather than destroy it.

GIVE BACK PRIDE

One of the ironies of corporations today is that they all act like losers. They have listened for so long to the mesmerising chant of the accountants to save a few dollars here, and cut a few dollars there, that they have forgotten that in many cases, they are wildly successful!

Of course any company in business works to make a profit but at some point, the penny pinching begins to eat away at the very being of the corporation. What has developed in the continuous rush to save money is that companies have lost their identities.

Many corporations have many very successful products that they should be proud of but pride is no longer part of the corporate culture. Perhaps pride was an expense that the companies couldn't afford!

How can one expect workers to do their best if they don't have pride in the company and its products. Of course, they can't! So a very important facet of creating a good employee environment is giving pride back! The concept of just working for a pay check may be enough at the subsistence level but most people also need a sense of pride in the work that they do.

One of the largest companies in a particular market placed used to have a strong corporate culture that engendered a strong sense of pride. That pride was in part for the products that the company sold and in part for the partnership that existed between the company and the employees. It was perceived that the company always treated employees fairly. Employees of other companies were envious because of the way that this company treated its employees. Unfortunately, that is all gone! Management turnover and business reversals have caused a serious decline in the way employees are treated. The "more than fair" attitude of the past has given to the "that'll do and if you don't like it - leave" attitude of the present. Of course, any pride has long since gone!

Pride costs nothing but lack of pride costs plenty! Any company that is serious about improving its competitiveness needs to give pride back to its employees. It can only do that by developing a relationship that is fair, and perceived to be fair, with its employees.

WHAT DOES THE COMPANY GET BACK?

When the employees begin to trust in the company again and they begin to come out of their mental trenches, they will begin to suggest improvements for company problems and ideas for new business opportunities.

Companies pay consultants huge fees to tell them the same thing that their employees have been saying all along but since the employees know the workings of the corporation intimately, they know all the flaws, and in many cases, how to correct those flaws far better than some outsider.

The key to a better and more competitive company is to create an environment in which employees will feel comfortable in developing better ways to conduct business and new ideas for new directions.

USE THE HUMAN RESOURCE

Many companies have not been using the most powerful resource that they have; their people! Untapped wealth lies in this sleeping resource that can only be realized by astute management.

It seems that past history holds many of the truths that companies seem to have forgotten. Some of the most important of these truths are trust, loyalty, and pride. These can only occur when corporate management genuinely cares and sees its workers as human beings with pride and feelings. **It is time that the bad times and the lack of trust be put behind and a start made that will turn corporations, (and their employees), from apologists to winners again!**

17. LEADERSHIP

One thing must change before any of the suggestions in the preceding chapters can be put into place. That thing is, of course, Leadership. Leadership, or the lack of it, is the reason that many companies are having, or will have problems brought on by downsizing. Unimaginative leadership in many companies has followed the allure of promised economic improvements that downsizing implies but does not deliver. As indicated elsewhere, poorly performing companies that are downsized are merely poorly performing companies with fewer people. Downsizing is at best, a retreat from growth to a temporary static or stationary state. In reality, corporate leadership has been short-sighted not to realize this fact.

Also, when considering the economic and social dysfunction that downsizing brings to workers that lose their jobs, one begins to question the ethics and morality of the leadership of these companies that would subject previously loyal and hardworking employees to such anguish.

The action of taking employees jobs away is hard enough in times of real financial trouble such as bankruptcy. Only an uncaring and callous leadership would take such an action unless it were absolutely necessary.

Business has always been demanding of its people. It robs them of time that they would rather spend with families. Also, like a spoiled child, jobs demand attention, to the exclusion of family, hobbies, and friends.

It has also always been harsh and often unfair. Business has no respect for feelings, for friendship, etc. As stated elsewhere, the only thing important in business is profit!

What is different with downsizing that some invisible line of fairness has been crossed. Perhaps it is the size or the magnitude of layoffs involved. Perhaps it is the seeming uncaring attitude of company leadership when downsizing is put into effect.

In the harsh world of business, it is ironic that both the ethical and the economic realities cry out against the senselessness of downsizing. In the future, people training to be managers and leaders of companies will examine the moral and economic bankruptcies caused by downsizing and marvel at the single-minded determination that led down this erroneous path.

To go from the sad state they are in now to the future, leadership in companies must change radically. All the things that have been suggested throughout this book can be done. In fact, most have been done and have led to long term success for those companies that have utilized these ideas. What must change before the first step is taken to improve efficiency and develop employee involvement is that leadership must stop being so focused on pennies that it loses sight of where the company is going and what is important.

What is important are the customers! It is so easy to become so focused on selling more widgets that one lets the quality of products or service slip. Soon fewer widgets are sold, so fewer people are justified. If continued, this becomes an economic death spiral until the weakened company folds its tents and departs into the sunset.

Next in importance to the customer are employees. They are the only force that can improve quality! Of course, thin the number of employees and even with the best intentions of the remaining workers, quality will go down. Quality is like a piece of string. At one end of the string is perfect quality, at the other is no quality. There is never perfect quality because that would imply developing a product until the window of opportunity is closed. But customers today expect and demand almost perfection in products and service. Any company that, for whatever reason, allowed the quality of its products or service to go down, would so find itself replaced by more astute companies that have maintained good quality.

Business is business. It is time that the leadership of companies recognizes that it is not the latest fad, be it downsizing, restructuring, or diversification, that will solve problems but the adherence to sound business techniques such as building quality products at a reasonable price that will do so. Of course, making the business more efficient requires a strong team of loyal and dedicated employees. Companies that think otherwise will have the fallacy of their thinking proven wrong in future economic battles.

Any major change implies that corporate leadership must understand and totally back any enlightened development of their human resources. Strong leadership is the key that must be in place before any change can develop. For some companies, getting the right leadership that can direct the company as well as encourage an enlightened employee program will be a major hurdle. In some instances, companies may have to shuffle their upper echelons of management to bring the strongest leaders to the forefront and move those less effective or with past histories of less strong employee concern. Efficiency and good relationships must start at the top. If they don't exist there, they certainly will not develop downward. Top management must be seen to be fair, honest and genuine.

The definition of a leader is one who conducts or guides by example. It seems that perhaps companies today need more leaders that concern themselves with the well-being of their subordinates. Astute leaders realize that like a well-led football team or army corps, that their employees too, can win over the competition. It is the leader's task to provide the morale and motivation for the employee force to enable them to do well.

18. REGAIN EMPLOYEE CONFIDENCE

Before a company can begin to fully utilize the benefits of a fully motivated and empowered workforce, it must first regain the confidence and trust of employees. In most companies in business today that will be a difficult task because of the various actions that have taken place in those companies in the last five to ten years.

Company downsizing with all the distrust and discontent that implies is not the only problem. The downsizing has often been accompanied by unreasonably high rewards for the top management of the company at the same time that lower level employees have had their pay increases restricted or frozen. This has created an environment of cynicism and lack of belief in management and in the company as a whole.

To redress the first concern, *all* employees' pay should be tied to company performance, not just the lower levels of employees. It is grossly unfair to reward upper management when penalizing staff at lower levels. Employees are astute enough to recognize this disparity and will not begin to trust the company until this basic unfairness is redressed.

As discussed in previous chapters, the next step to regaining employee confidence is to make a statement that the company will no longer follow downsizing / restructuring program under any normal economic situation. Further, a statement should be made that employees will be retained in all possible situations even if they are relocated to different areas of the company as economic situations demand. Of course, the first step of condemning downsizing is a necessity as employees cannot have trust in a company that will lay them off merely to improve the company's stock market position.

The second step of transferring employees or relocating them rather than laying them off may seem heretic in today's business world but considering the fact that it takes from a year to eighteen months for an employee to learn a job and all the company's policies and to develop a network of contacts so that he / she can function effectively, it makes economic sense for the company to retain all the good employees it can. It also reassures employees that their talents will be used even if it means a transfer. If an employee is transferred from one department to another, he / she still retains that knowledge of policies and of procedures of how the company does business that a new employee would have to master.

A transferred employee also still retains the value of any company training. Of course that training would have to be redone if a new employee were hired. A final, very strong reason for retaining employees is that you know, or should know, their strengths and weaknesses. All but incompetent employees should be retained. People who are not capable of performing satisfactorily should be dismissed or relocated to a less demanding position where they can perform satisfactorily.

In this first step, the company must develop a sense of security toward its employees. They must be made to feel and believe that the company will retain them if they do their job. This again flies in the face of current corporate thinking!

You need workers to make your corporation successful. They can either be a succession of poorly motivated people with little of the company's interest in mind or they can be highly motivated people that feel that their work has merit and who have the company's best interest as a deep seated guide to their work. It goes without saying which will make a company more successful.

The next step is to examine corporate policies to redress those that have negative impact on employee morale. In all cases that it is possible, these policies should be modified or improved so that employees can see that the company is trying to be fair to them. Policies that are fair are the surest way to regain employee trust.

An example of fairness is the way a poor performing employee is dismissed. Unless the employee needs to be removed for safety or security reasoning, there is leeway for treating them fairly. This could be allowing the employee reasonable time to search for a new position.

Very rarely is the cold-hearted instant dismissal called for, or necessary. Some companies have even had the security guards escort the dismissed person to the plant exit. Only persons involved in a crime or that are potentially dangerous should be removed in this fashion. The company is depriving them of their job, it does not need to rob them of their dignity as well!

People will work for a pay check but for most employees, the job is much more. A great deal of pride, accomplishment, and self-worth are derived from their job by most employees. Many people get their most important sense of who they are from their job. Even job titles are important and should not be changed or removed without serious consideration. The stroke of a pen can change in a minute what may have required years to attain. We need to understand and allow those feelings of esteem that go with job titles or job descriptions that imply advanced knowledge or abilities as they cost little or nothing to continue and may cause much dissatisfaction and feeling of less value or worth if removed or changed.

This security that is suggested in the steps above will free your employees from fear. Can you imagine how effective employees are when they are always concerned for their jobs? Certainly not as effective as employees that know that their jobs are secure if they do their work well. Fear of losing ones job is a motivator but it is a negative motivator. Positive motivation is much more effective!

19. Staff at the Correct Level

One of the most obvious ways to fully utilize the "human resource" is to staff correctly.

Of course, most companies have addressed the overstaffing in their company or have they? That depends if the reductions in staff actually trimmed excess employees from overstaffed departments or if, in fact, those "sacred cow" departments are left intact while some correctly staffed departments are reduced. When employees that were fully justified by the workload are laid-off, that workload that they carried still exists. It is merely wishful thinking that the remaining employees will take up the slack and handle the workload. Of course, to an extent they will but their previous responsibilities and workload will suffer because of the expanded workload.

Who will suffer most in an understaffed company? The employees with the higher workloads, the customer with lower quality products and service, or the company, as it loses customers? Without a crystal ball, the company cannot define at what point customers will have had enough and take their business elsewhere. Press too hard though and that point will be found!

This is an extreme form of gambling to see just how far customers can be pushed. It is extreme because management is betting that they can sense the fine line and stop the actions and policies that have caused dissatisfied customers before the customers desert in droves. Let us hope that management is right as they are betting their companies' futures on it. In today's competitive workplace there are always other options. Dissatisfied customers will find and utilize those options!

It may be that to staff correctly, companies will have to add staff to departments that were depleted because of incautious downsizing. The companies will only be able to do this when they realistically face the facts of excess overtime and abnormal shifts being worked.

If staff reductions are necessary, they should be very carefully planned and should impact revenue producing departments least. Any company that reduces revenue producing staff reduces its potential for future growth. As indicated in other chapters, whenever possible, internal transfers should be used in lieu of dismissing employees. Most companies have guidelines that use some revenue per employee comparison. If possible, a company should always staff at those levels if they are realistic Any attempt to run a company short-staffed is merely a short term policy that will give few, if any, real benefits when excessive overtime costs and overworked employees are considered. Any employee that must work too much overtime or doesn't have enough time to do their job correctly will carry a stress overload that will affect their work and their home life. Staffing at reduced levels also makes it much more difficult to deal with growth. Since employee staffing is not even adequate for current levels of business, new growth will cause even further problems. Training new employees to meet the increased demand of new growth will cause the existing employees to work even harder. This will cause continuously lower levels of quality than would be the case if the company staffed at the correct levels.

Consequently, as discussed previously, another real result of short-staffing is reduced quality of work at all levels. Even if one area or department is reduced below proper staffing levels, other departments that interface with that department will suffer reduced service, poorer quality products, etc.

If the short-staffing is more company-wide, the lowering of quality becomes more widespread. At some point, customers will detect this reduced quality, either by higher product failure rates, poorer service, or a reduced supply of spare parts. When customers perceive a lower level of quality, it won't be long before they will be looking for another supplier for the product or service that your company now provides.

As indicated above, a good indicator of understaffing is increased amounts of overtime work and decreased task completions. This should be taken as a warning sign that quality will begin to suffer. It is very easy to dictate lower staffing levels from headquarters by assuming that new products or technology has reduced the workload of remote employees. Often the reality is that even with new technology and products, many of the old tasks remain. Coupled with this is the more complex work environments that new technology brings that employees must deal with. Technology does not necessarily reduce workload, it changes it. It may even imply a higher workload to keep abreast of new hardware and software advancements. As mentioned, this more complex work environment often implies new and additional responsibilities that employees must shoulder. Senior management is often unaware of these tasks and additional requirements, either because these requirements have not been communicated or because management hasn't listened. Often the latter is the case as the push for reducing staffing levels often brushes rational considerations aside. In this case, most of the effort that management makes is to justify downsizing, not to rationalize against it! As indicated below, faulty statistics are often used as a basis for reducing employees or implying a reduced workload.

A good example of this occurred at ABC company. This company spent a considerable number of man hours installing one of its products. Since this was a one-time action for each installation, the company chose not to include the man-hours for these installations in staffing considerations. Consequently, staffing requirements were skewed because of this fallacy, ultimately leading to understaffing as the departments still had to provide the employees for the installations, as well as maintaining the existing workload.

This rationalization or modifying of statistics is unreasonable and is often used to improve the short term position of an individual or group or to justify previously held positions. It does not do the company any favors because it creates myths rather than reality to base staffing calculations on.

Using invalid statistics to determine a new policy direction or to make decisions can be dangerous! The reason that this is so is that a decision based on faulty or skewed statistics is not based on fact but some skewed perception of fact. It is not uncommon for people that want to force a decision in a particular direction to use facts that back up their case and ignore others that disprove it.

The example given in the paragraph above is such a case. Statistics can be crafted that often have little to do with the realities faced by the workers of that company. But because the statistics are supposedly "fact," they bear uncommon weight in the consideration of decisions setting new directions for the company. Statistics can be used or misused to make any case or to validate any course of action. It can be seen that over time, companies that use or are biased by faulty statistics, have an increasingly unreal grasp of the actual situations of their companies. It is easy to become mesmerised by figures and statistics to the point that important points become lost about the way the company functions.

For example, how do you place value on developing and maintaining good customer relations? It has absolutely no value if considered in the cold analytical light of statistics. It gathers no profit. Conversely, it may cost some small expense. Also, it could be considered as unproductive time if valued in the light of actual work accomplished.

Be that as it may, time invested in furthering customer relations is perhaps the most valuable time that an employee can invest in the long term success of his / her company. Without good customer relations, sales efforts are difficult, if not impossible. **It is never the last product sold to a customer that is the most important but the next!** Of course, a company cannot get to sell the next product if the customer dislikes sales or service staff or products. Strong customer relations pave the way smoothly from one product to the next.

From the above discussions, it should be realized that any company that purely uses statistical data to set manning levels and does not factor in the need for time to develop and maintain good customer relations is not staffing for long term success.

Continuing the consideration of staffing levels, employees still must take vacation, they still get sick, they have family emergencies that they must deal with. What happens is that customers of short-staffed departments suffer, be they internal departments or actual customers. Although customers may sympathize with whatever personal emergency causes a problem, they will still hold the company responsible for the same level of attention and service, regardless of the short-staffed situation.

Another item to factor in to the staffing calculations is to consider how many special projects or other work outside normal duties is required. The staffing levels can then be modified accordingly. One can pretend that these needs can be ignored but work emergencies dictate otherwise.

A company that seriously wants to staff correctly should consider historical data of recent time periods to evaluate past trends in this area as well as considering any special projects, etc., that will impact a department in the near future.

Staffing at the correct level is a very important decision and needs to be based on fact, not wishful thinking. People far from the day-to-day work often have considerable say in staffing decisions. As indicated above, unless their input is based on reality, these staffing decisions will often be wrong.

Companies need to take a serious look at the impact that excessive overtime caused by short-staffing has on employees' lives. Continuous excessive overtime and the related increased stress can cause marital problems, health problems, and decreased employee efficiency. No company should willingly impose those long term problems on employees.

An intelligent company would realize that employees that have the correct work load, perform better and can add more of their talents and skills to the benefit of the company and themselves.

The current corporate thinking is "do more with less." If the previous staffing level was correct and it is now reduced, the reality of the situation is "do less with less!" What really happens is that work is done less effectively and is more reactive in nature.

It seems enigmatic that at the very time that competition is strongest, that many companies hamstring themselves by laying off employees, who often end up working for the competitors. Talk about a motivated enemy: Consider an employee that feels that he / she was unfairly dismissed and that now works for a competitor! He / she knows all the previous company's weak spots and can do real damage just being a motivated employee of his / her new company!

I'm sure that customers notice the decreased level of attention that they receive from downsized companies. Once again this is a very important reason that downsizing is counterproductive; in the heat of the battle for the customers' business, some companies almost give their business away by decreasing the attention that they pay to customers. The competition will be glad to fill in for their deficiencies!

Some companies make the mistake of thinking that the customer must do business with them. They even develop an arrogance toward the customer. No company, regardless of its size or product, can succeed with this attitude for very long! This very attitude has brought some of the largest and most prominent companies to a very humbling loss of business.

If a company staffs at correct levels, employees can be used in innovative ways as suggested in other chapters. Employee morale and effort is highest in a company which is staffed correctly and that treats employees fairly. They will certainly put forth much more effort for an employer that they trust than one that they fear.

For the long term benefit of both the employees and the company, staffing at the correct level is the correct thing to do.

20. Develop a Strong Sense of Direction

In the last decade many companies have lost their way! They have gone from having a strong sense of what they do, where they are going, who they are, and what they stand for, to become directionless mammoths driven by stock market pressures. Many companies bought into the fallacies of downsizing, restructuring, diversification, and continued down that path until very little of their original direction was left. It is unfortunate that poor economic performance, or perceived poor performance, led to such major changes that much of which was good in the company, as well as some things that needed correction, were tossed out in the efforts to improve efficiency.

The changed companies have little resemblance to the companies that their founders had crafted. The statement that comes to mind that was used to describe these previous, more benevolent companies is "good corporate citizens." In a more enlightened age, many of these companies understood that the communities surrounding the workplace and the company were partners. The company provided jobs for the people and support to worthwhile efforts in the community. The communities provided people to staff the company and a good environment in which the company could prosper.

In the new economic environment of the last decade, thoughtfulness and consideration for neighborhood communities and for employees has largely disappeared.

It is unfortunate that many companies are not astute enough to recognize the error of letting outside pressures dictate the direction that their companies take. Just like teenagers following a new fad, companies have fallen in the same mindless follow-the-leader roles, following the lead of other companies in directions that often do little to solve the real problems of the company. As discussed previously, downsizing does not fix the problems that create poor economic performance, it merely applies a quick-fix bandage that often makes the economic problems worse.

Also another impact of downsizing has been to remove many managers from the company that had previously established a corporate culture that defined what the company was about. When most members of the "old guard" left, often so did any sense of "company family" or fairness. In many cases, their departure was intentional; that is, the new management wanted to mold the company as they saw fit, so obviously, these previous managers had to go! When they went, with them went much of the impetus that had led the company in a certain direction. The few remaining "old guard" either held their opinions to themselves or found other companies to use their talent.

Today, many companies regularly re-invent who they are and ignore the very core of their business that led to their success. Very often these changes of direction occur as they buy smaller businesses to develop into areas in which they have little expertise. In these newly purchased businesses, the rules for success are often very different to those that the managers are familiar with.

These diversifications have often led to poor economic performance and confusion. They have also caused much employee concern and dissatisfaction. This has been caused by poor direction and imperfect planning on the part of the management of the company. It is also caused by failure to listen to employee input about the problems caused and the solutions needed in the new business direction.

Any economic adventures should be thoroughly investigated and all facets should be considered before becoming involved. If these necessary steps are not taken, the diversion can lead to serious problems. Many times these economic misadventures lead to poor economic performance and a serious financial drain on the mother company.

Of course, the employees of the mother company have to adapt by tightening their belts to offset the company's economic errors. Employees very quickly equate the poor performance of a weak acquisition, quarter after quarter, to their decreasing levels of pay or pay freezes.

It is very hard to persuade the workers that management has a firm grasp on reality unless they see a strong sense of direction, purpose, and *success*! It is also hard to develop continuity without good long term management that understands the business and its people.

In this new environment home-grown management is relatively rare at the top of any company or corporation. It is the fashion to ignore internal talent and buy outsiders to fill the top spots of the company. Sometimes this works but often it is less successful. What is missing is the in-depth experience of how the company works and also the "growing up together" of the management and its employees. To new management, employees are merely numbers that, like chess pieces, can be moved across the board or removed as the whim takes them.

A company must have or must develop a strong business plan. The first step to developing this is to involve customers in the development of new products. As indicated elsewhere, this is the most cost-effective and wise way to set the direction of new development. This should also help set economic guidelines for the proposed cost of products so that these products can compete with competitors' products.

Another way to ensure customer loyalty, in addition to providing quality products and prices that both customers and companies find acceptable, is to develop innovative pricing of services so that long term relationships are developed with customers that provide more stable situations for both the customer and the company.

The next step in developing a strong sense of direction is to address the real problems in the company that cause poor economic performance. As indicated elsewhere, there are many problems that can be addressed that will cut costs and improve efficiency. Many of these problems can only be solved with the assistance of the employees. Improved technology can help but it is merely a tool that, if used intelligently, will aid in solving problems.

A further step that must be taken is to develop a consistent and fair policy in dealing with employees. Without this, all other efforts will have little long term effect. Companies must also have a good moral compass to lead them in the direction of fairness.

One thing that corporate boards of directors must begin to do is look to the long term good of a company and reward all employees rather than merely over-rewarding a few of the top corporate officers. The company is much more than just a few individuals at the top of a company! It is time that fairness and consideration for the rest of the employees again becomes important!

This reward may not necessarily need to be just in the guise of larger pay raises but also in better working environments and more even-handed treatment. To become more successful, just as companies involved customers to help develop long term direction, so must they involve employees. The employees must become partners in developing a new, improved relationship with management and then, helping the company implement those directions. Companies that resist this direction will weaken their abilities to compete, while companies that utilize their human resource will prosper.

No real sense of direction will be developed until companies accept that their employees are vitally important to long term company success. Once this vital step is taken, companies can begin to develop an environment that will reassure employees.

It is a hackneyed phrase but management must begin treating its employees the way that they would like to be treated if they were the employees and the employees were the management.

Work is much more than just a paycheck. People put much of themselves into their work. They take pride in their successes, they grieve over their mistakes. The longer that an employee works for a company, the more that they identify with that company.

A good indicator of where a company stands, both in terms of employee loyalty and trust in the company's direction is the pride that employees have in their company.

One cannot be proud of a company that one does not trust. Nor can one be proud of a company that does not have a corporate culture that engenders pride. Even a company that builds fine products, or provides fantastic services does not generate pride unless the company, by its actions deserves that pride.

Give your employees their pride back! Make them part of creating the directions that the company will take. Give them a strong reason in addition to a paycheck to feel proud. They've worked hard for it. Both they and the company deserve it!

21. Develop and Use Internal Talents

Today's average company has a good mixture of talent within its ranks. The most obvious talents and commonly the only ones that are utilized are the ones that fits each employee to his / her job. There is also a great deal of hidden or unused talent in the employee ranks. The reason that this talent is hidden or unused is because after the initial job interview and acceptance, the company no longer considers any of those talents. In fact, aside from the few facts on an employee's resume, the employee remains almost an unknown quantity. The things that are learned about employees such as work habits, attitudes etc., are valuable but are too often unused.

Adding to this lack of knowledge is the subjective information that is added by the yearly job review. Many companies consider these reviews almost valueless, particularly for employees that work independently.

These reviews either define employees as persons whose work habits only fall slightly short of sainthood, or other employees who barely are acceptable in the job. Of course, these evaluations are dependent on the subjective judgments of managers that may or may not be fair. Some employees abilities and skills fit well into certain jobs and others do not. These less well-suited employees may have talents that could be outstanding in other areas. If the company could discover these talents, both the company and the employee would benefit.

Not only do employee skills in the job and innate talents differ, so do their levels of challenge. Some employees are satisfied doing an acceptable job, whereas others can do their jobs and still desire other tasks to challenge them.

Is there a potentially good manager working as a truck driver? Is there a potentially outstanding technical writer working as a service technician? Is there a manufacturing technician that has the potential to be part of a design team? Is there a latent inventor working as a floor sweeper? As things exist today, no one will ever know and those latent talents will never be used, much to the detriment of both the company and the employee.

It is unfortunate that only college trained individuals are considered talented enough to have ideas. If one considers past history, one can discover many individuals that had little formal training but yet developed historic new inventions or came up with amazing new ideas.

Consider the resume of several brothers:

Job desired - design engineers for previously undeveloped scientific projects.

Skills - Basic mechanical and woodworking skills.

Educational levels - High school completed -- no diploma received.

Job experience - Currently own bicycle shop.

Other - Read a lot in areas of interests.

Of course, any corporation today would laugh at these credentials until they read the names of Orville and Wilbur Wright.

Today in our presumptuousness, we smugly believe that only the properly trained individuals can come up with earth-shaking ideas. How dare we be so dull as to ignore history! As in the past, there are people today in organizations that may have ideas that could revolutionize society. These people may not have the technical skills to bring these ideas into reality but the kernel of these ideas lie still-born in the imaginations of these individuals because companies have become so hide-bound in their thinking. This is the great final sadness of the twentieth century, that we have become so enamored with technology that we have ceased to encourage ideas.

Companies should encourage internal talent scouts to hunt out employees that may have other talents apart from being skilled in their jobs and develop growth opportunities for them. These talent scouts should also be on the look out for hidden talents and develop growth paths for the employees that possess these talents.

The reason that this is necessary is that many companies today have become stagnant in their abilities in encouraging employee growth and development. Many new middle or upper level positions are filled by outside hiring. This, of course, discourages existing employees and creates a cadre of outside talent that does not understand the importance of various functions within the company nor what has been successful in the past.

Change is an important and necessary constant in any company but that change should be coupled with an understanding of the corporate culture and the strengths and weaknesses of the company so that the company can succeed and prosper over the long term.

Too often the direction of companies are rudely jerked from the paths of past successes into less successful detours by management that isn't aware of all of the ramifications of the decisions that they make. Growing employees from within has the effect of taking employees that understand the company and the business that they are in very well and taking their talent to the upper levels of the company. This would help to keep management firmly grounded in the realities of the business.

A company needs a constant healthy growth of employees upward so that management has ideas that reflect changes in policies procedures, and knowledge of new technology that constantly impacts lower levels. If this growth does not occur, management becomes increasingly out of touch with the day-to-day realities of their company. This implies that more and more management decisions are based on a reality that is dangerously out of date.

However much companies may like to consider their employees as disposable commodities, the reality is that unless internal talent is utilized, company competitiveness will deteriorate.

Also, newly hired employees are even more of an unknown quality. The company does not know the various work traits that these new employees have. As companies progress, they will need more self-reliance, self-motivated, independent people to be able to compete and be successful. There is no better way to find these than to look for these talents in existing employees.

So aside from looking at employees' resumes, how could a human resource "talent scout" determine what skills the employee base contains? Obviously, the annual review on each employee should give some clue to the basic strengths that an individual has. These reviews could be modified so that the manager or supervisor could indicate other talents or skills that have been observed.

Also participation in focus groups and team leader assessment of skills brought to play in solving problems and developing new ideas should be used as indicators of potential in these areas.

As indicated above, one area that companies need to rethink is the place of higher education as the only consideration for advancement. Of course, in more technical areas, in-depth knowledge is required but often disappointing results occur when using just education as a controlling factor. In many countries, more importance is put on job performance, attitude, and willingness to learn and develop new skills, than an over - reliance of advanced education.

Another consideration for developing employee hidden talent is that if an employee has developed several secondary skills, that will make it easier to redeploy them into other areas if the primary skill becomes less necessary. That way, the employees' talent stays within the company, rather than benefiting another company.

Once steps have been taken to recognize secondary skills and talents, employees can be encouraged to use those talents or develop them. It may be that a hobby such as drawing or artwork, could be developed into an area that is needed by the company. An example of this could be creation of artwork for new products.

Another example could be an employee who works on the manufacturing line who is a good speaker. That employee could conduct customer tours of the production line. This would provide a more instructive and insightful tour than management conducted tours would. Another example might be a manufacturing technician that has talent in writing skills. This individual may be able to improve the level of technical writing on hardware products.

One never knows of the talents that may be available or could be gainfully employed and that are available within every company, unless these talents are searched for. The least probable employee could have skills or talents that could enrich and benefit the company, as well as the employee.

This is a challenge to the human resource departments to find what "human resources" really exist within the company, then to nurture and develop those talents. If you never look, you will certainly never find. Employees should be considered the "treasure chest of hidden talent," to be found, encouraged, and developed.

As companies become even more competitive, good labor will become more and more valuable as all other facets of a company are optimized. It will be realized that retaining good employees is very important. The training that employees are given and their knowledge of the company is an asset that costs a great deal to replace. Of course, every employee can be replaced but valuable employees with good attitudes and skills are difficult, if not impossible to replace.

How To Find Talent

The obvious question is how to prospect that "gem" of an idea or that hidden talent that is deeply hidden in the minds of employees?

If it is agreed that job evaluations do not give a totally objective picture of employee skill, it is obvious that these are of little value.

The first thing that companies can do is ask their employees! In some cases, employees may be aware of skills or supplemental talents and would be pleased to let the company know what those skills are.

The next level of the hidden or submerged talent is much harder to bring forth. Many employees, because of their low job level and perhaps low self-esteem, may keep their ideas or talents well hidden so that they are not subject to ridicule or worse.

If "idea" programs were developed that encouraged and rewarded "free" thinking by employees; more innovative ideas would come forth. Employees should be rewarded for *any* ideas, however ridiculous they may be! Only when such an atmosphere of encouragement is developed, will some of the deeply rooted ideas come forth. Fear and ridicule must be removed before "free thinking" will develop.

Summary

By using "talent scouts," companies should search out and develop employees with skills and talents, both latent and apparent. These developed employees should provide a flow of talent up through the company that could provide "new blood and new ideas" to supplement the management and technical skills that now exist. This flow of upward talent will provide a current reflection of reality at lower levels and should aid in making more sound and relevant decisions.

The development of internal talent sends a strong signal of the importance that a company places on its employees. It also benefits the company by aiding it in making more correct decisions, and the employee by providing scope for growth and development.

The company may have within its ranks, the employees with ideas and suggestions to make the company stronger and more productive. In fairness to both the company and the employee, these talents should be sought out and encouraged!

22. Use Talent Innovatively

To get the maximum benefit from the human resource of a company, new and innovative ways of using employees' talent should be considered. Once employees regain their trust and loyalty in the company, they will be willing to help forge a stronger company.

Every company has problem areas that slow the flow of business and create bottlenecks. As discussed in other chapters these problem areas will never be found until all employees become part of the problem solving equation. Any company management that labors under the misconception that management can solve all the problems without employee assistance is only deluding itself.

Presuming then, that companies realize the importance of utilizing their "human resource" and take steps to make their employees feel secure and regain their trust, how can companies benefit from the employee resource? Rather than just utilizing employees in the same old ways, companies must learn to use their employees' talent innovatively.

The first way is to develop flex-work standards if not already in place. Flexible working schedules, of course, allow employees to tailor their days so that they can miss heavy prime shift traffic situations. They also allow employees to schedule their work days to meet personal commitments, such as meeting children at school, etc.

The problem with flexible work schedules is that if not done correctly, some loss of control over work hours and quality of work can result. It is important before any flex-time scheduling is allowed, that a clear understanding exists between the worker and his / her supervisor about the amount and quality of work expected. Also, any mandatory time that employee presence is necessary should be discussed and understood. If the company is enlightened enough to consider flex-work, it should not suffer from lower work standards or unavailability of key employees.

Of course, in a shift operation where operations run twenty four hours per day, the entire shift system could be moved, (with employee consensus) to a more amicable arrangement. This way heavy traffic to and from work can be avoided. This flexibility in scheduling will remove much unnecessary stress from the work day and consequently, will result in more relaxed and more efficient employees. Flex scheduling and modifying shift start times are both no-cost steps that can be taken to make employees work-life easier.

With employees whose presence at work at a given time is not so demanding, arrangements such as pagers that pass on telephone messages and cellular phones can be used to ensure employees availability.

What may be necessary in some situations where it is possible is to rethink the standards of the job. Until now, the amount of time that an employee spends being present at his / her place of work has been more important than the work accomplished during that time.

What is more important than the time spent on the job is, of course, the quantity and quality of work completed. This concept may be anathema to many managers that consider punctual reporting for work of prime importance. The workers of the information age are in many cases already working many non-standard work shifts to accommodate the demands of their job.

Information system workers, for example, are called upon for telephone assistance or on-site assistance at any hour outside "normal" shift hours. Also a fair degree of night or weekend work is part of the normal job. These workers should not be held to the same time constraints as normal prime shift workers. The advent of cellular transmitters and receivers built into laptop personal computers means that employees can be at work any time or any place.

Self-discipline is required of workers that are allowed some leeway in their job time requirements. Also, a very clear understanding should exist between the employee and their supervisor as to acceptable and desirable levels of performance and tasks to be accomplished within given time frames.

The very traits that the new technology requires; that of self-motivation, honesty and good time utilisation are the traits that companies must encourage by providing a stable and fear-free environment.

Of course, there are employees that could accomplish all or most of their required tasks from home via a home personal computer. So long as the guidelines in the above paragraph are adhered to, the company should be able to get at least the same and perhaps better work from these employees. The key to a "telecommuting" worker being successful is availability! One never knows in the course of day-to-day work when the specialized talent of the "telecommuter" will be required, so he / she must be available to satisfy the needs of the company.

At this time, most companies are not very inventive when it comes to employee skills. They hire employees for a position and there they stay, even though that employee has talents in other areas.

It is possible with utilising these additional skills that these employees could continue to perform their regular job but could also act as advisors or utilise their experience to help develop new products or services. The technology is available but most companies are still thirty years behind in using that technology in adapting the workplace and employee utilisation to it.

An example of how workers with additional talents could be used: An experienced technician that recognises and suggests improvements could be part of a new product design team. This does not mean that he / she needs to change jobs, instead he / she could continue to do the original job, perhaps at a diminished level while spending part of his / her time working with a design team, either in person or via computer.

There should be some initial personal contact when the focus group is set up so that the members can develop personal rapport. During this phrase, the choice of group leader is critical! The leader must be able to fit together people with different skill levels and areas of expertise, as well as different personalities.

As indicated, the biggest problem in projects of this nature is selecting a team leader that "facilitates" the direction that the project takes by setting broad goals such as time frames and expectations then helps the group work toward those goals by listening, advising, and feeding back information. A good facilitator will not direct or micromanage the details of the focus group but, as indicated above, will focus on the broad details such as major goals and overall time frames.

After the initial meetings to set the direction of the project, regular tele-conferencing or video-conferencing or even a dedicated e-mail grouping can be the venue of the team. If the effort is made, many diverse skills can work together to develop more innovative and reliable products if the experience of past efforts is collected together.

One might say "why not just put the person on the development team and forget the e-mail or tele-conferencing." **The most important reason is that if you want to tap into a person's experience and utilise it, unfortunately, the moment that the person leaves a particular job, their relevant experience begins to date.** To be of continuing importance, experience must be current! After a year or eighteen months out of a position, the person's experience viewpoint is no longer valid because it has become dated.

A good focus group is a valuable tool that can be used to solve problems and seek solutions from a diverse group with common interests. Those interests have to include knowledge of the various facets affecting the focus group, problem areas and possible solutions to the problems. It provides a platform for resolving interdepartment conflicts by involving interested parties that understand the interactions between those departments and coming up with a workable solution that is amicable to both departments. This implies that the representative/s from a department are given the authority to make changes. In practice, the representatives feed back points of discussion to their management and carry back important points to the next focus group meetings.

Another innovative way to utilize employees talent is suggested in the chapter on "Develop and Use Internal Talent." Innovative companies that develop the ideas and skills of their employees that have been unused may have to be innovative in the use of these ideas.

For example, if an employee came up with an idea that was totally outside business areas that the company wanted to pursue but the idea was one that could be patented, the company could assist the employee in getting the idea patented. Of course, some amicable arrangement would have to be made between the company and the employee that would reward both by sharing any financial income from the patent rights.

An additional way that a company can be innovative in its use of employee talents is to be flexible in the use of technology for utilizing ideas.

Companies in general have become so infatuated with technology, computers in particular, that they perhaps have forgotten that computers are merely tools. Because of the infinite and virtually unlimited ability of computers to be of benefit in assisting in accomplishing work, and the fascination that many have with the technology, the demand has been strong to make people adapt to the computer rather than making the tool, (the computer), adapt to the worker.

Much time and effort must be utilized to learn and relearn computer literacy skills. Computers and the software on them, have not, and do, not encourage ease of use. Just look at the pile of manuals for the various programs and you will understand the point. The point being made is that computers must be made more intuitive to use so that less effort goes into learning and understanding the machine or the software and more effort can go into thinking and developing new ideas.

The more innovative companies may realize that some employees will be prevented from presenting or developing ideas because of the constraints of the computer or their lack of ability to use the computer. These intelligent companies will understand that more traditional means may be needed to encourage all employees with ideas to develop them.

Companies must not be so presumptuous to presume that only the "computer literate" have good ideas. As stated in a previous chapter, that "million dollar idea" may be germinating in the mind of a floor sweeper. It would be a shame if companies weren't innovative or broad-minded enough to search for, and develop such ideas.

Of course, the innovative use of employees as suggested above cannot happen if the company is so short-staffed that no one can be spared without impacting day-to-day operations. A department that is staffed correctly should be able to cope with an employee being unavailable for short periods. Of course, vacation, illnesses, and training also imply absence that must be considered in as well when setting staffing levels.

If employees are willing to carry the extra load that additional assignments imply, the company should reward them with bonuses, increased pay raises, etc.

Yet another way to use employees innovatively is to use them as "consultants" within the company; considering that employees know the market place and the company's products better than any outside consultant would, and considering that outside consultants would be much more expensive than using employees, it makes sound economic sense to use employees, and to reward them for their expertise.

As indicated in other chapters, employees that are not fearful about their job and that have trust and loyalty for the company will add to the competitiveness of the company. Of course, the more secure the company becomes, the better it is for all concerned.

Aside from the benefits that the company may gain, the employees will enjoy their talents being used more fully. The "human resource" is a resource that can be used to the advantage of the company and the employee or abused and ignored to the detriment of both.

The whole concept of considering the workforce as a valuable resource that can be used in many innovative ways is vital to companies striving to remain competitive. It has several important benefits. Of course it will help provide the company with better new products that are easier to use and less costly. It will also improve employee satisfaction and morale and will encourage other employees to become involved and think innovatively. It also develops the skills of the involved employees so that they become even more skillful and more valuable to the company in providing innovative solutions.

23. Grow Employees in Place

In the past, to grow within a company implied in most cases, a change of location, either to other cities or to headquarters. This is fine but only a limited number of employees could grow this way. In addition, with downsizing reducing the numbers of middle managers of companies and cutting other jobs at headquarters, the traditional flow of talented employees upwards has slowed to a trickle.

Also, more people are beginning to understand that constant movement is not good for their family's happiness or well-being. More employees are passing up promotions so that their children can have a more stable school and home environment.

These employees also weigh their current environment with the environment in larger cities and all the additional factors that implies; such as higher housing costs, higher cost of living, poorer schools, higher crime rates, and longer and more difficult commuting. In many cases, the added costs and the decreased standards of living, for many weighs against relocation.

Companies must come up with plans and ideas to utilize the talents of the upwardly mobile, ambitious employees as well as the employees that have consciously chosen to stay at a lower level for family and personal reasons.

If some path for growth is not provided for the ambitious employees, at some point they will leave the company and join another that will provide them with that avenue for development.

Also, additional ways should be developed for the stay-at-lower-level employees. These may be the best and brightest employees with the most to offer their companies. In both cases, some new ways must be developed to use and grow these talents or they will both be lost to the company.

Recognizing talent and utilizing it where it is can provide the opportunity for growth and development of talent wherever it may be.

Telecommuting

Some companies have begun to allow some employees to telecommute to address some of these issues. If the employee is self-motivated and understands the importance of being available and if the company provides firm guidelines of acceptable work levels, this can be very productive. Without the distractions that are present in most offices, most home workers can work harder and more effectively than they could in an office environment. Of course, some degree of office attendance keeps them abreast of current developments as well as providing the social interface that is so necessary to be part of any organisation.

For the appropriate jobs, some degree of working from the home will become not only acceptable but expected. An added benefit is that having more employees working from home, is that the company will require less office space. The biggest problem standing in the way of home-working is the mind set of current managers. The idea of "if I can't see you, you're not working" must change! Managers must learn to evaluate workers on work accomplished, not physical presence.

As telecommuting becomes more common, it will force change in the way that the work time is considered. For example, if an employee has a computer at home and can accomplish some facets of his / her job at home and the rest at an office or customer sites; time spent in the office becomes less important. Task accomplishment is more valid as a yardstick to evaluate employee merit than strict adherence to time standards. Most workers can recognise that there are employees who are very punctual in reporting to work and who are very precise in completing the administrative minutia, but are far less valuable than other workers that are less punctual and less precise in administrative detail but put out better quality and quantities of work. In some cases, the choice is an employee that puts in time or an employee that gets things done.

In addition to telecommuting, there are many additional ways to utilize the talents of employees remote from main offices. Of course, as indicated in earlier chapters, the secondary skills that employees have must be known to be used. So, as indicated elsewhere, the company must search for employees that have talents that can be used.

Focus Groups

One example of the way that employees could be used are as members of focus groups. As these focus groups go through their problem solving or idea development phases, some individuals will stand out as objective thinkers that add much to the discussion.

These employees should be encouraged by recognition and reward. They should also be included on other focus groups until they can be trained as facilitators or moderators of focus groups themselves. Of course, focus groups most often function by holding occasional development meetings in a central location but conduct most of their work via teleconferences. Of course, with the advent of the Internet, chat groups can also be used as well.

New Product Testing

In addition to focus groups, remote employees could test new products and provide unbiased feedback on their operation and suggestions for improvements. Many times it is important to have persons that have not been involved with the design and development to test products to see how the product stands up when used by a novice that is unfamiliar with it. This is important because most customers that use a product are, in effect, novices, at least until they become familiar with it.

Training

Also, another way to use remote employees' talent is in training. For those that have skills in this area, that talent could be used by training them formally on a new product such as a new software package. On their return to their remote offices, they could conduct training courses and train other employees. This could be done in a seminar to teach several people at once or as an on-the-job training effort conducted one-on-one with another employee. To make the training effective, it should have clearly defined goals and levels of competence expected. This would also have the effect of reducing training costs as well as growing talent in the field.

Course Development

Another way to use employees with skills in training and experience in a particular field is to utilize their skills in course development. Currently, in many companies, course developers are often unfamiliar with the levels that use the training that they develop. In many instances, current courses provide few of the necessary skills that are needed because of the course developers' lack of knowledge of the skills needed.

In this instance, it would be very appropriate to involve employees with current in-depth knowledge in the area of proposed courses to assist in the development of new training.

Verification of Technical Procedures and Publications

Another example of ways that employees could be grown in place is by verification of technical procedures and publications. Often these are written at a level that causes confusion and frustration to the user or customer.

A good example would be the operating procedures of the VCR. Many customers just use the most basic functions of the VCR because the operating procedures are often complex or confusing. Employees verifying, simplifying, and correcting instructions such as these before they are published could provide more easily useable products as well as reducing publishing costs.

Planning

Another way to utilize remote employees' talent is to have them become involved in planning. Often planning involves communicating, organizing, discussing issues, and making sure that resources are available to accomplish work.

The ways to use employees that are remote from headquarters or large offices are limited only by the imagination. This has the benefit of using employee talent where it is to make company products more effective and also to develop employee talents.

The more innovative companies will meet the challenge of finding hidden employee talent and will begin to utilize that talent. The less competitive companies will find such innovation too dangerous or too complicated and will continue to stagnate where they are.

The adventurous companies will satisfy employees needs by understanding that not all employees can or want to gravitate to headquarters but may be quite happy where they are. These employees may have talents and ambitions that can be used and satisfied, respectively.

These companies will come up with ways to utilize these remote employees so that both they and the company benefit.

24. Eliminate Excessive Administrative Work

Unfortunately, administrative work is often over-valued and actual work that benefits the company is under-valued. Companies that seriously wish to improve their competitiveness must decrease the amount of administrative work to that which is necessary and streamline it so that it can be quickly and easily accomplished, leaving more time for beneficial work.

Every manager or person that is in a position to add administrative tasks should be taught that each added little administrative detail can accumulate with other little administrative details to the point that employees spend more time addressing administrative details than working. Each manager, supervisor or person in a position to add administrative requirements may individually have small requirements. It is when all these cumulative requests from different sources are added together that the administrative requirements begin to overload employees.

Eliminate Incremental Add-On Tasks

One of the most insidious thefts of employee time is the incremental add-on task. Many people within a company pass on tasks that are not really the responsibility of the addressed individual. These tasks are often in the area of "if you did this, my job would be much easier."

Some people are very good at delegating various facets of their jobs out to the point that much of their job responsibilities are being done by others. This causes increased workload for others and should be discouraged. This situation can be resolved by holding a discussion with the "delegator's" manager to set up working rules that will eliminate informal delegation of tasks.

A very good example of this was the major effort made by a company to eliminate redundant requests for information and reduce administrative tasks by the development of a comprehensive new data base. This data base took many hours of development by many employees from all different disciplines within the company.

The program was explained to all and it was agreed that any information that was required could be retrieved from the corporate data base. Within six months, requests were being made and actions requested that were in direct conflict with the aims, goals, and design of the system.

The point being made is that regardless of how well designed any agreement may be, human nature will try to undermine it! It requires constant vigilance to prevent misuse and undermining of efforts made to streamline administrative work.

It should be stressed that *no* person should add administrative work without upper management approval. Some companies do not realise that they are administrating their employees and their companies to the back of the competitive pack! Excessive administration work is like an anchor, dragging employees and the company down. The task then, is to free your employees from all unnecessary administrative work and make the accomplishment of necessary administrative work easy and fast.

Eliminate Incompatible Computer Data Bases

For example, a common way that computers cause excessive administrative requirements is by the company computer having incompatible data bases that cannot share information, requiring multiple input of similar or peripheral information. If common data bases are used that share information, a single entry of data should suffice.

ELIMINATE UNNECESSARY INFORMATION

Another problem that computers have caused occurs because it is possible to store increasing amounts of data, hence more and more data is saved and available for decision making, (and confusion). It is possible to have too much data! In companies' rush to make sure that all data is available, many have provided too much to their employees. The result is confusion and even slow decision making because no one can keep abreast of the flood of information available today.

What is needed is an in-depth evaluation to determine the level and extent of information that is needed. All departments should determine exactly what information they need to do their jobs. They should also indicate how long the information is needed. The reason that this is necessary is that much of the information needed in a company is of a temporary nature. It is so because it may be valid today but invalid tomorrow because of change. Other information is more long term in nature, for example weekly, monthly, or yearly.

When the validity is determined, the computer system can be developed to erase data that is no longer valid. Only required information should be provided and vigilance should be applied so that redundant, outdated, or useless information is not stored or provided.

UTILIZE AVAILABLE TECHNOLOGY

Companies should also take note of some of the techniques used by retail stores. Rather than using the time consuming and error ridden technique of hand entering data about parts transactions, these parts should have the scannable bar codes that contain the part number and asset number. That way, entries on parts usage would be much quicker by scanner and more accurate. Also, that could cut down on response time required to replenish depleted stocks.

As indicated in other chapters, another way to cut down administrative time required is to have personal computers smart enough to contain the intelligence of the particular data entry requirements so that much of the work can be done at the level of the personal computer. This would reduce the time required to input data by allowing this to be done at the PC level. When the work is completed, the PC could then communicate with the central processing unit automatically, passing the information at high speed.

This would free the employee from wasting time going through the communications hook-up phase and also the waiting between each transaction before being allowed to continue with the next phase of inputting data. This single change would cumulatively save thousands of hours of wasted administrative time per year.

Another thing that could be changed is to have personal computers automate repetitive but necessary tasks. For example, rather than time being wasted doing repetitive "saves" to make sure that the work one is doing is saved, an "autosave" program could be put into place that would automatically save data on a recurring basis. This would eliminate the time employees waste taking care of this task and would also prevent inadvertent loss of data if power were lost, etc.

Along the same lines, if computer hardware and software designers could develop automatic personal computer back-up programs that ran during times of low or no usage, all data that was on the PC could be protected by "backing it up" to another device. This way no data would be lost if, for example, if the personal computer's hard drive became defective and was no longer accessible. This would save all the time needed at present to reload or re-input data.

STOP DUPLICATION OF EFFORT

Another way to eliminate excessive administrative work is to stop duplication of effort. Why have all your employees rediscover the wheel? By this I mean, if the solution to a problem is known, make sure that it is communicated to all that it might affect. That way, no time is wasted searching for a solution that already exists.

Along the same lines, since most companies are in constant training on new equipment and software, rather than making the untrained employees struggle through using a new hardware or software product, have a trained person train the remainder of the employees. Some people do very well as trainers and when such an individual is found, their talents should be used and rewarded. Not only will this reduce the time spent struggling through problems, it may prevent costly mistakes.

Expanding the idea of new hardware and software; whenever possible make the new product an incremental extension of the old. In other words, rather than employees having to go through a total new learning curve, have new products that build on previous knowledge or experience. This would cut down the training required and give employees a greater comfort level. This is always a good training technique even on new products. Go from the known to the unknown by discussing the similarities and differences between old and new. Once these are understood, the unique qualities of the new product can then be discussed.

SUMMARY

Briefly, it is important to reduce excessive administrative work because, of course, this wastes effort, time, and money. It is also frustrating for employees doing unnecessary tasks because they realize the futility involved. Workers laboring under the weight of excessive administrative details will be unable to complete their normal tasks as expected and consequently will suffer from a much higher stress level than is necessary. If administrative work is streamlined so that employees do only what is necessary, they will be freed up to do more productive work. Their job performance will certainly be higher. If employees are freed from the yoke of excessive administrative tasks, they will have more time to work in some of the more innovative and rewarding ways as suggested in other chapters.

If companies are to use the "human resource" to the fullest extent, they must reduce administration tasks to the required level and constantly be on their guard to prevent over-tasking to creep in and steal time and talent.

25. ADD EMPLOYEES TO YOUR MANAGEMENT TEAM

Every company has many problems that must be resolved if it is to become more competitive. Some of these problems are large and visible but many, if not most, are small, niggling, and invisible to upper management. Just because they are small and invisible does not mean that they have no impact! These problems are like burglars in the night, stealing the wealth that the company produces in a thousand hidden ways.

One could observe that, if these problems are small and invisible, they obviously cannot be solved. That is the catch, they may be invisible to upper management but there is someone at some level that knows about these problems. The key to their solution is, of course, getting the persons involved that are aware of the problems. Once they are brought to light, they can be solved.

The average company today does not involve its people in problem solving. First, it has created an atmosphere of fear and insecurity that dampens any employee desire to solve problems. Secondly, management of many companies has evolved into an attitude that, in their wisdom, they will solve all the problems of the company and they don't need any input, thank you!

This second attitude is a condensation of many of the ills of current companies. Management, without employee assistance cannot resolve a company's problems. To think otherwise is merely a delusion.

Any company that wants to become and stay competitive, must first create an atmosphere that will encourage employee involvement and then solicit employees' assistance to define and then resolve the "hidden" problems. If a company really wants to improve, it must enlist the assistance of its employees!

This is not just the inclusion of employees in some "super" suggestion program, this suggestion is the direct involvement of employees in the direction of the company. The question should be asked, "who really knows about the problems of a department, a manager that has not been involved in the work process for a number of years or a worker that is involved daily?" The answer is obvious!

The sad thing about management is that as soon as a good worker is elevated to manager or supervisor, his / her currency or direct knowledge of the job begins to dwindle. The longer that the manager is away from the first line job, the more out of touch that he / she becomes.

There is only one way to get the immediacy of current knowledge in making decisions. That way is to get workers direct input while they are still working at the job! Intelligent management should understand this and involve employees that have ideas or suggestions and that can express themselves.

This is, of course, a major change from today's environment and requires strong and intelligent management to make it work. This has been done before, most notably by Eddie Rickenbacker while he was general manager of Eastern Airlines. If any company wants to replicate the twenty five years of success that Eastern had while Eddie Rickenbacker was at the helm, it should utilize the ideas that Eddie used. These ideas are timeless, they will work just as well now as they did forty years ago for Eastern.

Management that recognises the need to use all their employee assets to make the company better will also be clever enough to create meeting environments that are not stacked against the employee contributors. An intimidating meeting that is full of powerful managers may not be the best place to put an employee or employees from lower levels. That is, not until some ground rules are put in place that reassure those employees.

The first rule is to give employees time to prepare so that they can discuss the points that they want to make. It may be well to provide assistance, not on the content of their discussion but the presentation and rebuttal of probable responses. That way the employee-presenters can make their points in a factual and confident manner. This will give the employees and their ideas the benefit of a fair presentation.

An important factor in soliciting employee advice is the selection of employees. The employees that are selected should have good ideas and have strong enough convictions so that they can put their ideas forward and stand up for those ideas. The last thing that is needed is an employee that is fearful or insecure to the point that when the ideas that he / she proposes meets with some resistance, that the employee just caves in to that resistance.

It may seem anathema to some managers to bring some less polished and forthright employees into the elevated levels of the conference room to help solve problems and provide solutions. To be frank, who cares who comes up with a solution, so long as it is a good solution? Managers that try to solve all their company's problems are like the lead mules in a twenty mule team. With only two mules pulling and eighteen mules just walking, the wagon won't move fast or far.

It is probable that the companies that get their employees involved and make them part of the management team will prosper and pull ahead of the competition while other companies that just keep searching for the "magic" restructuring that will cure all their ills will founder and fail.

Using employees as part of the decision-making process will not guarantee success because for the concept to be successful, it presupposes that upper management is enlightened enough to want it to work. Also, it will require a "sea-change" in the attitude of existing management to even consider the possibility, let alone to provide the unswerving support such an idea requires to succeed.

For too long companies have labored under the delusion that only management should have input on decisions and the higher the manager, the more important his / her input is. It is sad that this has developed, for the potential for real problem solving or new ideas often lies outside the management structure. **Using employee input may be the key to solving many of those problems that management does not even realize exists**. Is the upper management of most corporations enlightened enough to support such a radical idea? An added benefit of using employees in this way is that new talent will be developed that can be added to the management structure as attrition creates the need for new managers. This will provide a proven source of innovative people with exactly the talent that the company needs to grow and prosper.

It is sad that companies get involved in "fads" just as teenagers do. In the eighties, the fads were "quality circles," the beginning of restructuring, and the "demise of the mainframe CPU." These fads are usually short-lived in most cases as reality proves that the fad does not provide the solution that was promised.

This certainly was the case in the "demise of mainframe CPU's." As more companies switched more of their processing from mainframes to servers, it was found that the promised savings did not materialize because of the hidden expenses implied in the support of servers and PC's. Also the "fad" was disproved by the failure of the servers in terms of robustness, reliability, and security.

The "quality circle" is a good idea but the strong emphasis that was placed on it by many companies some years ago is now not so prevalent. Quality is not a one-time fix, it is an ongoing process that only becomes really successful when companies become innovative enough to make it succeed and make it a continuing part of their policies.

It may be that employee involvement in management will become the "fad" of the next century as more companies try it and find that it succeeds beyond expectation. Be that as it may, whatever the cause, employee involvement will become part of the policies of many successful companies.

26. Make Ethics a Cornerstone of Your Business

If one examines the business world today, one quickly realizes that something is badly wrong with the decisions being made. Business has always been competitive; there have always been sharp or unscrupulous managers and business leaders. The thing that is different today is that many companies, that in the past, were icons of corporate fairness, are now involved in many of the same selfish and unethical acts as the lowest level of corporate pirates.

For example, take the example of a corporate officer addressing company employees: "Ladies and Gentlemen. Over the last ten or fifteen years, the management of this company has hired a few too many people. You may have noticed these people walking around aimlessly. Well, we sort of messed up. We're not sure who was asleep at the switch, and allowed this over-hiring but there you are.

Now the accountants and the stockholders are raising Cain! So, of course, something must be done. Now, some of the other managers and I sat down and thought about it after lunch the other day. We put our heads together and thought and thought until we came up with *it!* What *it* means is that someone is going to have to pay! We drew straws and unfortunately, you all lost! Please return and clean out your desks and you will be given your checks as you exit the building. By the way, management thanks you all for volunteering to leave, otherwise something really nasty might have happened such as some of us might have been fired because we over-hired two thousand people."

Another example at another company; as the chief corporate officer addresses an employee meeting: "Ladies and Gentlemen, as you know this has been a good year for our company. We finally got rid of that company that we bought four years ago as a little economic adventure that, to be quite frank, turned out to be a financial disaster. I don't know what we were thinking about when we bought it, I guess that we were so overcome by the pretty company logo that we didn't investigate the finances enough. I looked at my horoscope and it said it would be okay so I thought, what the hey, and I, or should I say we, bought it. I know that you have had to pay by taking pay cuts to make up for those massive financial losses but hey, it was for a good cause.

Luckily, that is all behind us now. But that brings us to the point of the meeting today. The accountants and our stock analyst have been pushing me to do something to get our stock out of the basement. I think they were just afraid of going to the next stockholders' meeting. I think that the key point that got my attention was when the company stock analyst advised me how much money I would make if our stock doubled in value. As you know, it takes a lot of money to pay for all the maids and servants at all of those houses that I have.

Be that as it may, I, or rather we, decided that something is going to have to be sacrificed to make the stock go up. First, we thought of selling the fleet of corporate jets but then that would mean that the corporate officers would have to fly with common people, er, on commercial airlines. Then we had a brainstorm! We thought our employees were getting bored with their jobs so we thought that we would do them a favor and solve our problems at the same time.

So I knew that you're all excited to hear that you all will be departing on a new adventure. As of one o'clock today, you are all going job hunting! We have set up outprocessing lines in the cafeteria. For your convenience we have set up many lines, so there will be no waiting. In your termination package, I have included a signed picture of me and the top corporate staff thanking you for your many years of devoted effort for the company and wishing you good luck in your new endeavors. The staff and I wish to thank you for leaving so we can make some more money and keep our jobs."

The above were two tongue-in-cheek looks at the cold new world of corporate downsizing. Although both were written in a light-hearted vein, both examples have been replicated again and again in deadly serious actions in companies across this country, as good skilled employees with much experience found out that they were without a job, a paycheck, and benefits. Of course, no manager is as frank as the ones in the examples. But what they said is implied by the realities of actual downsizings.

These examples were not meant to make fun of people downsized out of jobs because that is a disaster at a very personal level and has much impact on the affected persons and their families. Instead, the examples were given to highlight the total lack of ethics that has crept into many previously high-minded corporations.

In the past, in more ethical times, managers would resign if their decisions led companies down the wrong financial paths. Today, it seems no mistake is large enough to cause upper management to accept the responsibility for, and the consequences of, their actions.

It is hard to think of a more unethical and selfish action than that of depriving good employees of their jobs merely to move stock prices up. As many companies have found to their discomfort, aside from being an unethical action, in many cases it has turned out to be rather stupid, as many key employees were laid off that were vital to the efficient operation of the company. Consequently, quality has plummeted in many of the downsized companies.

For companies to get well again, ethical standards need to be put in place that restore responsibility to management, and honor to boards of directors and corporate officers. The first step in regaining the trust of employees is to re-create the ethical behavior of corporate officers that was once common currency in the companies that were held up as icons of American business.

It is time to come out of the shadows and back into the light. Competition is hard and will continue to get harder. The companies that strive for the higher ethical ground will regain the trust and loyalty of their employees and grow stronger. The companies that continue on a low ethical plane will lose the remainder of their good employees to more ethical companies and grow weaker.

27. SUMMATION - WHY CORPORATIONS WILL STOP DOWNSIZING

Restructuring, downsizing and reorganizing are all euphemisms for laying off employees. Previously, the reasons for downsizing have been discussed. As mentioned before, downsizing causes many negative things that in turn cause long term problems and a few short-term positive effects. If the impacts that these actions cause are primarily negative in nature, what will stop corporations from this continuous cycle of blood-letting?

UNIONS

It will probably not be the unions! In most cases the unions' power has decreased because of the concerns about corruption of members or potential members, because of companies relocating from the strong union area of the Northcentral and Northeastern states to the largely non-union "New South" states, and because of companies relocating to off-shore countries. Global competition has played a part in reducing union power as well. The FAA controller's strike that President Reagan broke by firing all the striking controllers, signaled the end of major confrontations between industry and unions, although unions still go on strike to gain their demands.

The laying off of thousands of workers just to improve the quarterly financial performance of companies would have once mobilised unions to rightly protest this unfair and unjust action. Just when unions are most needed, they appear as powerless to stop this latest trend. Having said this, job security is becoming a larger factor in union discussions and actions as more union members become concerned about their long term prospects.

Much of the reason that unions have not had more impact is, of course, that many of the affected people have not been in unions. Many of the people that have been laid off are white collar, middle class workers that traditionally have not been union members so unions would have no reason to become involved. These people previously may have considered the union movement with disdain, as something that working men were involved with. Now, with no united structure of any type to support them, these middle class, white collar workers can be displaced from their jobs at the whim of their companies.

POLITICAL PRESSURE

By itself, political pressure will not cause corporations to stop the practice of downsizing. To begin with, there is a limit to how far government can go in defining how companies can run their business. There is also the difficulty of defining the difference between real layoffs that are necessary to keep a company in business, and artificial layoffs just to improve economic positioning. It could be argued by companies that if steps are not taken to reduce employee levels, that their company would be in a poor economic position and would fail.

Rather than getting involved in these difficult and tenuous areas, the government could be more successful by rewarding companies that do not reduce staffing levels by reducing corporate taxes of those companies, thus giving companies economic rewards for retaining employees. Either the government rewards companies with good staff retention practices or it pays for unemployment relief to support employees that have lost their jobs.

MEDIA-PRESSURE

Although an effective tool, media pressure by itself will not bring an end to company downsizing. First, efforts are too disjointed to have the effect that they should. Also, it is very hard to focus attention on a problem that, in many cases, is spread over a wide geographic area. For example, if XYZ Corporation downsizes its operation, it may lay some workers off at headquarters but the majority may be laid off in many different geographic locations. Because of the geographic spread, it is very difficult to gather sympathy for individuals that are laid off. What collectively may be a major catastrophe for the workers of a company; when viewed from the outside, the problem may seem small and isolated.

Also companies may use the guideline of performance as a means to eliminate people. This gives the semblance of a logical dismissal of poorly performing employees, when in fact, it may be the mechanism used to lay-off many highly paid workers and later replace them with lowly paid novices. In most cases, performance factors are subjective and often have little relationship to the value of the employee to the company or the work that he / she does. These performance factors are often weighted toward administrative tasks that are of questionable value when viewed from the perspective of relative worth to the core business that a company is in.

Another thing that can confuse workers and outside observers is the fact that standards can be defined to create a performance structure that ensures that any employee can be laid off. For example, a company could define three performance levels, unacceptable, marginal, and acceptable and then restrict the use of acceptable to hand - picked individuals, so that most employees fell in the marginal or unacceptable level. Then, when employees are laid off, it could be said it was because of poor performance.

Another way that poor performance can be used to lay off people is to take the lowest performers in each office. Of course, each work place will have its "totem pole" of employee performance. This is the natural but subjective ranking of the workers in top, middle, and lower levels of performance and has no real relation to other offices. So the company could just lay off the lowest performer of each office or could pick a level below which all employees would be laid off. Because a level of performance that one office may consider outstanding may be considered average at another office, this method is very subjective and unfair.

Another confusing factor for outside observers is the fact that current performance reviews reward conformance and often the very people that a company should want to retain are not conformers but adventurers. To be successful, a company should understand that it must have a mix of conformists and adventurers. If all employees are conformists, very little innovative thinking or actions will take place. If all employees are adventurers, there would not be enough control as everyone would be going off in different directions. Companies, by demanding that employees conform tightly to behaviour and control standards, first identify, then remove adventurers. This is sad for both the company and the removed individual. Very often, the adventurers are the best and brightest people with the most innovative ideas and any company is poorer because they have not discovered ways to use the non-conformists' talents. Again, a mix of adventurers, (thinkers), and conformists is necessary for the best chance of success.

Of course, a company should be able to remove individuals whose work is sub - standard. Any person in this category are not normally the ones whose jobs are eliminated. The employees that are most impacted by layoffs are the ones to whom the lay-off comes as a surprise. Up to the time of being laid off, very often the worker has no reason to be concerned about his / her job. So far as they are concerned, their job performance is satisfactory. If it were merely poor performers that were laid off, there would be little sympathy or concern amongst the remaining employees.

What companies have done is to break the unwritten, unspoken agreement that employees at least understood. That is "so long as I do my job well, the company will retain me." "If I don't, I understand my job is in jeopardy." This is no longer true! Too often good people that have done good work for companies are being laid off! This is the single most damaging impact that downsizing has on the employees that remain!

What all these variable and sometimes confusing standards do is to make it very difficult for an outside observer to make value judgments on the correctness or fallacy of dismissing downsized workers. Of course, the media would have a very difficult time voicing more than quick thumb nail sketches of laid off employees and media presentations would have very little depth to the realities of the downsizing. One must understand the company, its business, and its strong and weak points, as well as the relative worth of employees downsized out of a job. Everything is relative and although an outside observer can view actions and events, they cannot place value judgments on those actions and validly assign rightness or wrongness to them.

The market place however does very explicitly reward good business practices. It rewards good customer service or well priced products with increased market share. It slices through rhetoric and the fog of confusion of poor business practice like an avenging sword, giving reduced market share to poor performers.

It is not true that all companies with the largest share of their particular market are good but for a company to remain at the top long-term, it must do many things right. So, if media is to have an impact on the way companies conduct business, it must spend time and effort to understand and then to explain and compare the *good*, successful companies and the not-so-good, less successful companies. The viewing, reading, and listening public is very concerned where the downsizing tactics will take them and this country. The public understands that downsizing companies lay-off workers that either cannot get new jobs or that must accept jobs at reduced pay levels, ultimately resulting in lower consumer demand which leads to lower company profits, etc.

The media can however, keep unrelenting pressure on companies that are down-sizing. By questioning each company on each downsizing, the media may cause companies to rethink their plans. By placing the downsizing in a negative light and discussing the massive personal distress that they cause, the media can be useful in limiting companies from rampant, unjustified downsizing. **The worst thing that society can do is to accept these pronouncements of corporate downsizing calmly!**

The business acumen of any company that resorts to massive downsizing should be questioned. If one examines the business realities, one would ask the following questions:

- "Did your company allow massive over-staffing and have you just discovered that fact?"
- "If not, if these employees were justified work and cost-wise before your down-sizing plans, is it true that with fewer workers, the level of quality of your company's work will suffer?"
- "Are you saying that your customer is less important now than before your downsizing plan?"

These are important questions that should be addressed to any company that is downsizing.

Another sound tactic that the media can play is to give in-depth coverage of successful companies that have not downsized. It would be instrumental to examine how these companies react in time of company economic decline; to find just what steps they take and how they utilise their *Human Resources* during those times.

EDUCATORS

Another area of influence on irresponsible downsizing is education. The Professors and teachers that are involved with teaching the prospective managers of the next generation should teach the reasons against downsizing. They should understand that long term growth and economic success has little place for downsizing. Of course, this will have little impact on the current rash of downsizing but may create a more secure future for both corporations and employees.

BUSINESS REALITY

The primary reason that downsizing will fall into disfavour is that, aside from short term positive effects on a company's financial health, *that it has major long term effects that are difficult to recover from.*

Once enough companies have traveled the downsizing road and

learned that it is not the cure-all for business shortcomings and when this information is passed on by the media, business papers, text books, and technical papers; companies will stop resorting to downsizing except in times of extreme company financial hardship, such as chapter 11 bankruptcy.

Here are some of the business reasons that companies will stop downsizing:

1. *It creates a disjointed organisation and creates inefficiency*. If employees are removed from needed positions, the work that these employees did will either be done by someone else or not done at all. In the case of another employee assuming the work, if that employee has additional tasks, that means that the new job responsibilities will not be covered as well. The new tasks must be learned and the network of contacts that are needed to do the job must be re-established.

One can imagine an organisation with many interconnected dots, each dot representing a person and their area of responsibility. Now if you remove a large number of those persons, you have created a number of lost links in the organisation. It is understood that jobs can be consolidated and that positions can be eliminated. However, **if the position was genuinely necessary before downsizing, it is still necessary after!** By the stroke of a pen, a position can be removed, however, the work that the position implied still exists and cannot be removed! Either the work will not be done or will be done poorly with fewer workers. **The first result of downsizing then is a lowering of product and service quality.**

2. *By laying off good people, the organisation is hurt far more than can be justified by any short term gains*. A company should be very careful even in a Chapter 11 lay off situation to only eliminate non-producing or low producing employees. Other employees recognise and understand poor performing individuals being laid off; they do not easily accept or understand when good employees are laid off.

What happens when good employees are removed from their jobs is that all persons that are cognisant of that person become disenchanted with the company. Lack of trust to the company spreads like an epidemic. When the layoffs become widespread, a general malaise sets in and affects most workers. Less voluntary work takes place, less enthusiasm is apparent and overall job quality goes down.

A good analogy is a football team. If a couple of good linemen are removed for no good reason, everyone on the team is affected. The team still plays the game but everyone has to work harder. Now the quarterback gets sacked more often but the coach blames the team. Soon the team just goes through the motions and eventually, the game is lost.

3. *Employee morale becomes severely depressed* - As indicated above, when employees perceive that good people are laid off, they begin to question the company's motives. They also begin to question their chance of long-term employment.

When a respected coworker is laid off for little or no reason, every associate of that person recognises the unfairness involved. This creates a loss of trust in the company and eliminates any belief of future fairness in company actions. It is though the innate sense of right or wrong that most people possess has been subverted.

In a single unfair action, the company can create more bad feelings, lack of trust, animosity, and dissatisfaction than ten good pay raises or twenty positive actions can overcome. It is though the company is intent in sowing the seeds of its own destruction.

Every action that a company takes, whether large or small, must be fair and must be perceived to be fair, otherwise that action will have negative connotations and reactions. A company's employee morale is like a pampered prize plant that has been nurtured until it is strong and hearty. An unfair and unnecessary downsizing has the effect of throwing weed killer on the flourishing plant; which now withers and sickens in spite of heroic efforts to revive it.

Lack of trust, suspicion, and fear, are all factors that de-motivate employees. So now on top of letting good employees go and the higher workload that may imply, the company is also faced with a severe case of poor employee morale.

Of course, the company will never know because in the fearful and uncertain environment that has been created, no employee will be brash enough to step forward and complain. So what exists is a case of the "The Emperor's new clothes." In other words the serious problems that exist will not be communicated because everyone fears for their position. **Vital**

feedback to the company will be reduced or eliminated by the fear created by unfair dismissals.

4. *Downsizing creates a pool of highly motivated ex-employees that any competitor would be wise to hire.* If you were a competitor and wanted an employee that knew all the flaws of the downsized company and would work strongly to win business away from their previous employer, you would be wise to hire an employee that has been downsized out of a job.

Often these employees have knowledge and a network of contacts within the company or knowledge of ex-customers that will give a competing company insight into the previous company's line up, business contacts, and areas of weakness.

A keen competitor should take advantage of this "gift" from the downsizing company and use it to gain competitive edge!

5. *Downsizing also creates much lower employee loyalty in workers that are still at the downsizing company so that astute competitors will find it much easier to hire key employees away.* It could be considered unethical or piracy to directly try to hire these employees but many times the disgruntled employees will approach your company first, particularly if you have hired employees that were downsized out of a job. These employees will feed back information about your company to their previous coworkers. If the information that they feed back is positive in nature, your chief problem may be to select the best of the workers now applying to your company. Canny competitors will utilise these new employees to gain strength, (and market share), from the downsized company.

6. *Downsizing almost invariably causes customer dissatisfaction.* Every action that a company takes that cuts down efficiency and creates higher workload and decreases employee morale; ultimately affects the customer, either by poorer service, poorer product quality, or both.

In the highly competitive arena of today's business world, reduced customer satisfaction can very easily lead to invasion by competitors and reduced market share. The one thing that does not exist in business today is a vacuum! In any case of reduced attention or lessening of customer satisfaction, an astute competitor will edge in and take advantage of your reduced attention to gain more business.

Although it does not necessarily follow that downsizing leads directly to less market share, many of the factors that downsizing causes can directly or indirectly contribute to exactly that.

7. *Downsizing thus weakens the company at a time that any weakness strengthens the competition.* A company's employees are a large part of its assets and should be treated as such. As no company would willingly hand over its new products or its key design engineers, or top management, nor should it hand over its trained and skilled employees. It should recognise employees' value and work to retain them and maintain their morale at a good level.

To draw an analogy, a company downsizing for the wrong reasons is like a platoon of soldiers going into battle. The weaker the platoon's morale and the lower the skill level of its soldiers, the less chance that it has to prevail when thrust into the heat of the battle. Likewise, to prevail in the heat of strong competition, the company must retain its *Human Resource* strength to succeed, it must not give it away to the competition.

SUMMARY

It will take a combined effort on the part of government, media, educators, and peer pressure to stop unwarranted company downsizing. It is time to stop companies from inflicting injuries on themselves and their employees. The companies can ultimately recover but in the wake of their recovery are countless unnecessary broken dreams, and distressed families of ex-employees.

These downsizings are not good for the employees, they are not good for the companies, and they ultimately are not good for our country. It is the taxpayer that must ultimately foot the bill for unemployment checks for the displaced workers. It is time that the myth of downsizing be put to bed and the realities be discussed. *Once companies realise the long term impact that downsizing can have on their business, downsizing will be viewed as a last desperate act to save a company in serious financial trouble.*

28. CONCLUSION

To summarize: This book has dealt with some of the things that a company or corporation could and should do to improve competitiveness and reduce any need for laying off staff. Some are very mundane, such as adhering to good staffing policies and reducing the money that is owed to the company to a minimum by streamlining collection and monitoring functions.

Some are almost beneath consideration such as corporate officers striving to stay ahead of competitors. Any failure to do this would result in decline and failure or take over by outside interests.

Some are more adventurous, such as enlisting employees to help the corporation solve its problems. These are the most innovative and hold the most promise because, until now at many corporations, employee involvement has been unwanted, and unused even though it holds the key to untapped savings and earning potential.

So your corporation has restructured yet again with less than desired positive results. You have applied all the suggestions in the first section and have seen some positive results but you feel that there must be something more that you could do to make your company more efficient and more profitable!

The previous section had several suggestions leading in the right direction. All companies have a valuable resource that is largely untapped. In the future, the companies that learn to utilize this resource will become more productive and more competitive.

The resource is not a product or products nor a service. The resource that companies will begin to utilize better are its employees. Most people would reply "we use our employees fully now!" Maybe you do but probably you don't.

Is your company a place that employees come to work charged up, ready for another days work? Does it provide a place that employees <u>enjoy</u> going to work? Do your employees feel an integral part of the company or just a cog in a big machine? Are your employees encouraged to be innovative, are they allowed to cross borders and think freely to improve the company? Or does fear, insecurity, anger or dissatisfaction create a "foxhole environment" where workers keep their ideas to themselves and keep a low profile while corporate barrages fly overhead?

In all but a few companies, fear, insecurity and concern are the order of the day. Ask how they feel and your employees won't be honest - they are fearful of the corporation and the blatant power it has over their jobs. The current corporate environment is one of fear and distrust.

This is not new! In 1934, Eddie Rickenbacker became the general manager of the fledging Eastern Airlines. As general manager of the airline, Eddie, with little formal education, took the company through twenty five profitable years. He did so by involving his employees in the company. When Eddie took over, in his words "morale was right on the ground." "For years there had been no continuity of management." "Every six months or so a new president or general manager would come in, add to the confusion and depart." "Personnel on the managerial level, up and down the line, had learned to keep their mouths shut and their costs down if they wanted to keep their jobs." "No one stuck his neck out with a new idea for fear the he would get his head hacked off."

If that is not a snap-shot of most companies today, I'm wrong! But since I have worked for and been involved with some of the large corporations, I know that Eddie Rickenbacker's words are a sad echo of many corporations today.

A well known political statement of a few years back was "it's the economy, stupid!" That should be revised to "its the employees!" A correctly motivated, charged up work force can drive your company into a stronger financial position as well as making a more secure and enjoyable workplace for employees.

This motivation has to be more than a brief seminar that is quickly forgotten! It must be a "sea change" of attitude and environment, starting at the very top and filtering down to every level of the organization. Also, it should be seen to be happening by actions rather than bold announcements and proclamations. You can tell people that something is going to happen but most will adopt a "wait and see" attitude to see what really happens.

All the things that you've heard about at management seminars, read in books and attempted to put in place won't work unless the entire company embraces and practices all of the policies, not just for the short term but for the long haul.

All companies have hidden talent just waiting with ideas and suggestions but in an atmosphere of suspicion and fear, these ideas remain unseen and unproductive. Give employees an environment that positively encourages involvement and removes fear, and the ideas will blossom forth like new flowers.

Much talk is about concerning "open environments" talking about computer access. What companies really need is open environments where people feel comfortable with addressing the problems of the company with free and open discussion with the company's interest in primary focus. That is what Eddie Rickenbacker did! He involved people at all levels of the company and he listened and used good ideas and encouraged people to use their talents. Even if Eastern Airlines had not developed pay and benefit schemes to encourage workers to stay with them, they would have anyway.

Workers are often frustrated in their jobs because the corporation hires them, puts them in a small box called "job description" and forgets that they may have other talents or ideas.

The human resources department should have talent scouts just like professional sports do to recognize and encourage the development of talent within an organization. In many cases, a company is better off developing internal talent to fit a position rather than hiring because of several factors. A new hire is an unknown quantity! The company really doesn't know what it has purchased for some time. It is better, when possible, to take a highly motivated person with willingness to be trained and train them rather than hiring an outsider. Another factor is the amount of time that is needed to familiarize new employees with the "corporate culture" of your company. It also takes new employees a long time to develop a network of contacts within the company and to learn the most effective way to conduct business.

Developing internal talent will fill the position with a known quantity, it will encourage people to work harder because of the potential for internal promotion and it will send a very positive message to other employees.

Motivation is the engine that can drive any company to dizzying heights of success. De-motivation is the anchor that will drag down the strongest and most powerful efforts of any corporation.

ADDENDUM

Additional Reading.

For those readers that are interested in reading more about Eddie Rickenbacker's management philosophies and how he built Eastern Airlines into an airline that was profitable for the entire twenty five years that he was general manager, please read:

Rickenbacker by Edward V. Rickenbacker.

BIBLIOGRAPHY

Rickenbacker, Edward V. *Rickenbacker - His own story.* Prentice Hall, Inc. edition published October 8 1967 Published by Fawcett World Library First Fawcett Crest printing, May 1969 - Chapter 11 How to Build an Airline - page 225.

GLOSSARY

BUY-OUT ---- The term used to describe a package that a company provides to its senior employees to buy-out or make financial compensations to them so that they will leave the company and can be replaced by more junior employees at lower salary levels.

BUZZ-WORD ---- Words that are used as a form of insider "short hand" to describe the latest trends or directions in a particular industry.

CORE-BUSINESS ---- The term used to define the central revenue producing function or functions within an organization.

CPU ---- Central Processing Unit. The main computer within an organization that controls all processing and services smaller, more localized computers and other attached peripheral devices.

DOWNSIZING ---- The reduction of staff within a company or corporation to improve profits or increase stock market performance of a company's stock.

FAA ---- Federal Aviation Authority. A government agency that is responsible for all rules and regulations governing aircraft, their use, maintenance, operations as well as pilot training, licensing and regulation.

GESTAPO ---- The secret police of World War II Nazi Germany.

HARDWARE ---- The computer equipment that is comprised of the central computer, its peripheral equipment and any other equipment.

ISO 9000 ---- A quality standard set by European Common Market countries that must be met to do business in those areas.

LOG-ON ---- The term given to gaining access to a computer by utilizing some procedure to ensure security of that computer.

MAINFRAME ---- The term given to the main or central computer of an organization.

MICROMANAGEMENT ---- The term given to a manager that gets involved in trivial details that would be better left to lower level management.

MIS ---- Management Information Systems. The name given to the computer department and its associated functions.

"MURPHY'S LAW' ---- A series of semi-humorous sayings, one of which states that state that "if a thing can be done wrong, it will be."

OPEN ENVIRONMENT ---- In the computer world, open environments imply the ability to connect dissimilar computers together to accomplish work.

OUT-SOURCING ---- The term used to describe the practice of moving a function from a company's in-house department to an outside vendor or contractor.

PC ---- Personal Computer - A smaller computer that is used by one or more persons to accomplish work.

PERIPHERAL ---- Hardware equipment that is attached to a central computer that performs work.

SERVER ---- A smaller computer that "serves" a relatively small group of attached computers or associated equipment.

SOFTWARE ---- The programs or written instructions that operate computers and peripheral equipment.

INDEX

A
accounts receivable, 17
administrative work, 141, 142, 144, 145
Alaska, 71
answering machines, 28

B
bankruptcies, 104
bankruptcy, 73, 74, 97, 103, 161
bureaucracy, 43

C
cash flow, 7, 15, 16, 17, 79, 83
commodities, 125
company family, 99
compartmentalization, 47
competition, 153
computer literacy, 133
conversations, phone, 32
core business, 8, 157
Corporate America, 86
corporate efficiency, 44
corruption, 155
cost of living, 135
cottage industry, 61
course development, 138
CPU's, demise of mainframe, 150
crime rates, 135
customer / supplier agreement, 48, 49
customer advisory boards, 70

D
Dale Carnegie Course, 86
data base, 31, 37, 38, 39, 40, 63, 142
decentralization, 16
development team, 49, 132
documentation, poor, 57

E
economic growth, 5
effort, duplication of, 6, 16, 47, 144
employee assets, 148
employee talents, 133, 139
employment, 62, 162
engineers, 47, 65, 71, 124, 164
ethics, 103, 153

F
FAA, 155, 173
finances, 61, 152
Florida, 56
focus groups, 126, 137

G
game playing, 39
Germany, 173

Gestapo, 11, 173

H

hard shell, 75
hardware and software, upgrade of, 41
housing costs, 135
human resources, 83, 84, 105, 127, 167

I

income, 18, 19, 133
industry and unions, 155
Internet, 39, 137
investment, 99
ISO 9000 certification, 89, 173

J

job changes, 62
job training, 138

L

Leadership, 103
licensing, 173
loyalty, 87, 101, 119, 120, 129, 134, 153, 163

M

management, upper, 33, 44
media pressure, 157
memos, 29, 30
merger, 45
micromanagement, 23
migration, customer, 73
mistake, perceived, 53
monopoly, 75
morale. low, 85
Murphy's Law, 56

N

networks, 58

O

open environment, 174
overstaffing, 5, 6, 111
overtime, 6

P

patent rights, 133
pay raises, 120, 134, 162
peripheral, 174
piracy, 163
political pressure, 156
power struggle, 16, 27
presentation, standard, 31
product testing, 137
profit, 3, 5, 13, 15, 20, 31, 45, 68, 83, 87, 88, 99, 103, 114

Q

quality circles, 150
questionnaires, 29, 30, 34

R

raw materials, 69
reading, 169
recession, 8
regulation, 173
remote employees, 66, 113, 137, 138, 139
restructuring, 5, 6, 23, 43, 44, 45, 95, 104, 107, 117, 149, 150
revenue, 5, 8, 16, 17, 18, 19, 22, 31, 74, 112, 173
revenue control, 17
Rickenbacker, Eddie, 93, 148, 166, 167, 169

S

sales and service, 16, 75
sales meeting, 33
server, 174
shift work, 59, 62, 130
short term savings, 92

standardization, 16, 57, 60
stock market, 5, 6, 11, 43, 73, 85, 108, 117, 173
stress, 54, 55, 58, 59, 60, 61, 62, 65, 85, 112, 115, 130, 145
strike, 11

T

takeovers, 26, 45
talent scouts, 124, 128, 167
technical procedures, verification of, 138
technology changes, 63
teenagers, 118, 150
telecommuters, 63
telecommuting, 136
telephone conferencing, 27
telephone skills, 77
transportation, 16
trench warfare, 95, 96

tribalization, 47, 48, 49

U

unemployment, 156, 164

V

vacation, 114, 134

W

web surfing, 39
work force, 11, 166
workers, contract, 8
working conditions, 59
world market, 5
Wright, Orville and Wilbur, 124